PRAISE FOR

Ask Now the Beasts

ᘓᘐᘔ

"You don't have to live with dogs or horses, backpack in the
wilderness or stay at a raptor center to be totally beguiled by this
vivid book. Rudner writes unsentimentally but with true sentiment
about a wide variety of creatures—falcons, seals, penguins, coyotes,
bears, even gorillas—to say nothing of dogs she has loved to the
ends of their lives. Horses are everywhere in these pages, patiently
serving in pack trains and under saddle. And they are also at liberty,
galloping joyously across their open spaces, pure grace in motion.
Pure grace in motion is how I see this fine book."

—MAXINE KUMIN, Pulitzer Prize winning poet,
author of *Jack and Other New Poems*

"Here are spirited stories from a woman who follows animals
with the wise eye of her heart—from Antarctic penguins to
Yellowstone wolves and coyotes, from a bewildered dog in Havasu
Canyon to brave peregrine falcons and bald eagles. Whether she is
snubbed by ducks, sure-footedly guided by her horses, enchanted
by a newborn gorilla, or frightened by a boxer dog named Yogi—
Rudner speaks for all of us who cherish interspecies kinship:
'It is *not* anthropomorphizing to fall in love,' she writes. 'It is
simply falling in love.' An inspiring and life-giving book."

—BRENDA PETERSON, author of *Build Me an Ark: A Life with Animals*

"Ruth Rudner is a writer of breathtaking sweep. In these pages, she writes, with brilliance and wisdom, about what really matters: the connection between people and the rest of animate creation. Whether she is showing us how to pull a string of mules, or how a peregrine falcon brought her the sky, every one of her stories surprises with shocking beauty and timeless truth. I read this book in one sitting, but will continue to think about her words for a very long time."

—SY MONTGOMERY, author-swineherd,
The Good Good Pig: The Extraordinary Life of Christopher Hogwood

PRAISE FOR

A Chorus of Buffalo

࿇

"Rudner's reverence for the magnificent creatures shines through her descriptions of firsthand encounters."
—*Publishers Weekly*

"The appearance of *A Chorus of Buffalo* may be the most important wildlife publication of the year. Rudner gives us an intimate portrait of America's quintessential animal."
—DOUG PEACOCK, author of *Grizzly Years*

"Required reading for anyone who wants to try to understand this magnificent animal and its role in the past, and complexities of its role in the present and the future."
—ANN ZWINGER, natural history writer,
author of *Downcanyon and The Nearsighted Naturalist*

"In her lyrical and informative *A Chorus of Buffalo*, Ruth Rudner makes clear that if we cannot find it in our hearts to continue allowing a place for this heart-stirring monarch of the plains, as goes the bison's fate, so likely shall go ours."
—DAVID PETERSEN, author of *Ghost Grizzlies and Elkheart*

"*A Chorus of Buffalo* is filled with emotion and passion from individuals and organizations on both sides of the preservation issue."
—*Outdoors Unlimited*

"A powerful, clear story about the evolving relationship between buffalo and people, and the ongoing struggle of the former to find some corner in the American West to roam."
—TED KERASOTE, author of *Navigations, Bloodties, Heart of Home, Return of the Wild,* and *Out There: In the Wild in a Wired Age*

"At once wise and compassionate, incisive and eloquent, Ruth Rudner's beautifully written meditations on the past, present, and uncertain future of the definitive western animal—*Bison bison,* the American buffalo—give us the beast in all its complexity and glory."
—T. H. WATKINS, late Stegner Professor of Western American Studies, Montana State University, and author of *The Redrock Chronicles*

"In a voice as bright and clear as the Big Sky, Ruth Rudner has created a moving epiphany to a comeback critter we the people, once upon a time, almost wiped from the face of the Earth."
—JOHN G. MITCHELL, author of *The Hunt*

"Ruth Rudner's eloquent and moving portrayal of the modern American bison teaches us how to stop thinking of this spectacular animal as something that happened in our past, and start dreaming about what it should mean in our future."
—PAUL SCHULLERY, author of *Mountain Time* and *Searching for Yellowstone*

RUTH RUDNER has written about the American West for many years, for *The Wall Street Journal*'s "Leisure & Arts" page. Her other books include *Partings; Greetings from Wisdom, Montana;* and *A Chorus of Buffalo.* With her husband, the photographer David Muench, she is also the author of *Windstone* and *Our National Parks.* Her work has also appeared in the *New York Times, USA Weekend, Field & Stream, Vogue, Self,* and many other publications. She frequently travels to and writes about America's national parks and the wildlife that inhabits them. She lives with her husband in Corrales, New Mexico.

ask now the beasts

ALSO BY RUTH RUDNER

A Chorus of Buffalo

Partings

Greetings from Wisdom, Montana

WITH DAVID MUENCH

Our National Parks

Windstone

ask now the beasts

Our Kinship with Animals Wild and Domestic

RUTH RUDNER

MARLOWE & COMPANY
NEW YORK, NEW YORK

ASK NOW THE BEASTS: *Our Kinship with Animals Wild and Domestic*
Copyright © 2006 by Ruth Rudner

Published by
Marlowe & Company
An Imprint of Avalon Publishing Group, Incorporated
245 West 17th Street • 11th floor
New York, NY 10011–5300

AVALON

Library of Congress Cataloging-in-Publication Data
Rudner, Ruth.
Ask now the beasts : our kinship with animals wild and domestic /
by Ruth Rudner.
p. cm.
ISBN-13: 978–1-56924–388–6
ISBN-10: 1–56924–388–3
1. Human-animal relationships. I. Title.
QL85.R83 2006
590—dc22
2005036195

9 8 7 6 5 4 3 2 1

DESIGNED BY PAULINE NEUWIRTH, NEUWIRTH & ASSOCIATES, INC.

Printed in the United States of America

For Blue
For Champ
For Ace and Lion and Flicka
For Rex

the stories

❦

ask now the beasts

introduction

ALL MY LIFE I have wondered what it feels like to be a horse, to come into the world and discover you are a horse. To be born into a landscape you will never question, to come out from your mother, stand up, look around and discover you are on the ground and the sky is above you and that you can walk and you can run. Oh, how you run . . . I think my only chance at that kind of understanding is to return—next life around—as one of them. Or maybe I *was* a horse in an earlier life and what I translate as curiosity is actually memory.

Once, in yoga class, my teacher said that humans were the most highly evolved beings. I took exception to that. Perhaps my feeling about horses leads me to it, but I believe some souls choose to trans-migrate into new lives as animals in order to teach, surely as evolved a calling as there is. "But ask now the beasts and they shall teach thee" goes back to Job, although humans have been learning from animals ever since division first appeared between us.

"Animals, like people living and dead, are teachers, protectors, destroyers, bearers of extraordinary perceptions . . . [they] are endowed with souls, and they are respected, imitated, sought, and consulted," writes Sy Montgomery, speaking of "other, older cultures than our own, in which people live closer to the earth," in her extraordinary book *Walking with the Great Apes.*

Certainly, the animals with whom we live become our teachers as well as our playmates, guardians, children, confidants. We learn their language, and, in learning, increase our ability to understand the language of all animals.

Maybe my teacher merely meant that we are the top of the food chain. Nobody would dispute that, even though that just makes us the only animal nobody needs. Or, is that what the height of evolution means? That we are beside the point?

Nothing survives for long in isolation. Once, in the Galápagos, I watched an iguana sunning himself on gray rocks a little back from the beach. The biologist with our small group told us it was the sole surviving male of that species on that particular island. There was one female of the same species—on the far side of the island. The two were divided by a steep, high rock ridge, something neither iguana was apt to climb. Biologists had decided that to take one iguana to the other would be to interfere with nature. Watching the male lying in the sun, we were watching the end of a race. How alive loss looks, I thought, watching him.

Each new foal I see in a pasture becomes an intensely personal moment for me. I am overwhelmed with curiosity. Is curiosity another word for connection? Many people are currently exploring our connection to animals. I read book after book about this (and watch endless animal films). It is as if writers, seekers, healers, biologists, philosophers—and an assortment of other people—are reaching out to establish a new (old) way of being. There have always been such people, but what inspires this now, in such numbers and in so active and public a way?

Maybe the seeking comes out of our having isolated ourselves in so many ways, building unclimbable ridges out of war, bigotry, greed, ignorance, fear. The more isolated we become, the greater becomes the activity toward connection. Like a pendulum seeking balance. If our neighbor will not come to the fence, perhaps our neighbor's dog will.

Animals have no urge to destroy us simply because we are different from them. As long as we enter their world with respect, we are (usually) safe with them. Respect is the operative word. A few years ago, a Yellowstone buffalo—who had probably had it with tourists pointing and shouting, crowding in with cameras, blocking buffalo passage across roads—gored an innocent bystander who had, in fact, been doing none of these things. But the bystander *represented* the lack of human respect the animal had experienced in his years in the herd. Each of us represents all of humanity. The question is, how do we want to do it?

Most of us connect with animals, consciously or not (and regardless of what we think about animal consciousness). We drive vehicles called Jaguars, Cougars, and Rams. We call our school sport teams Wolverines, Bobcats, Grizzlies, Panthers. (At least in Belfry, Montana, there is a logic to the team's name—the Bats.) The stuffed animals I played with as a child have real lives. As an adult, those same toys contain memories of connection to the *animal* as much as to the toy. They are symbolic of what I once knew as real. I connect to the cause of saving panda habitat because my childhood stuffed panda went everywhere with me. Why would I abandon it now? The cuddly stuffed buffalos in my bedroom form a herd that, in my imagination, becomes the free-roaming herd I cannot contain.

Animals brought into nursing homes or children's hospitals often reach withdrawn or angry or frightened people no one else can reach. Near the end of my father's life, when he felt isolated from all of us, angry, and frightened by his isolation, I often found him sharing a banana or a cookie with my dog Blue. (Once he tried to give him a lemon drop, but I interfered in that one.)

The captive lions at the MGM Grand in Las Vegas, Nevada, draw enormous crowds, even though they rarely do anything but sleep. (I watched an attendant throw a beach ball over and over at one lion, trying desperately to get it to do *something*. It just wanted to lie down.) People line up in great numbers early in the morning to get their pictures taken holding a current lion cub. Hunting magazines frequently picture a fierce, mouth-open grizzly on their front cover, intimating that the hunter himself is up to the fierceness. Warriors of the Plains tribes—according to the great Crow leader, Plenty-Coups, quoted in Frank Bird Linderman's book *Plenty-Coups, Chief of the Crows*—traditionally ate of the grizzly bear's heart because the grizzly is "always in his right mind, cool-headed, and ready for instant combat against any odds, even when roused from sleep. . . . to eat of the raw heart of the grizzly bear is to obtain self-mastery, the greatest of human attributes."

Not long after I moved to Montana, where I lived for many years, a friend shot a black bear and invited me for bear steaks. At the time, afraid to backpack in the state by myself because I imagined a grizzly bear standing behind every tree, I decided that ingesting bear, even a different species, would ward off being ingested by bear. I felt that eating bear would provide me some of its power and its spirit. (It took a few months of backpacking to understand that sightings of grizzlies are relatively rare, and that it was a great privilege to see one in its own country. Even so, I felt the bear power and spirit were useful attributes to possess.)

That bear meat was not my first intimate moment with a bear. I grew up with the skin of a black bear my hunter father shot in the Adirondacks before I was born. Its face was as familiar to me as any in my family. For years I crawled around the house on hands and knees with the bearskin over me, believing I had become the bear. Was I playing? Or was I participating in some private, instinctive ritual of spirit?

Adults who still wear fur may consider they are buying luxury, but once swathed in fur, can they be free of the animal whose coat it once was? Is there a subliminal lure to fur clothing, something beyond display of wealth? Aren't we fiercer wrapped in leopard skin than in wool? Those who protest the killing of any animal for the luxury of its coat are also fierce in their animal protection/connection. Antihunters and ethical hunters all bear the same love and appreciation of the animal hunted, although perhaps the hunter, keenly aware of the animal's world, its biology and habitat, is closer to the life of the animal. Predation is as much an act of life as the song of a canyon wren.

For sixteen years I walked my dog Rex in New York City's Riverside Park. The intensity of connection every dogwalker in the park felt with his or her dog was palpable. Recently I decided to make a concentrated study of New Yorkers and their dogs. Sitting on the stoop of a New York apartment building facing Riverside Park for an hour, I watched people and their dogs walk past. *All* the people looked like their dogs. That might be called narcissistic, but I think it is connection, a sort of transspecied way of being in the world.

The list of ways we relate to animals is endless. Sometimes misguided, sometimes biased, often exploitative, often truly caring—in a way, it is all the same thing. A longing for connection. When, in national parks—usually in front of a sign saying that feeding wildlife is prohibited—people throw out the crumbs of their picnics or open bags of chips to throw to birds and squirrels and, whatever else happens past, they probably believe that by feeding the animals they gain connection to them. There is a wish to be involved in an animal's life, to identify with it, to somehow be *seen* by the animal or *as* the animal. To be gentle as a dove or a baby lamb, fierce as a lion or a grizzly bear. To fly like an eagle, swim like a fish, run like a cheetah. To be loyal as an old dog, fast as a thoroughbred, agile as a cat.

I have spent my life with animals. Some are domestic animals with whom I have lived. My dog Blue and my horse Ace appear in a number of these stories. Born into a household with dogs, I saw them as fully a part of the family as my parents and my brother. I had no idea there were differences between us. We all belonged together. Those dogs, as well as Blue and Rex, Ace and Lion, and all the other animals with whom I have shared a domestic life, form a bridge—for me— between domesticity and wildness. Becoming "speakers" for the animal world, they bridge the gap between "us" and "them." There are differences between domestic and wild animals, but the similarities are greater.

I have been lucky enough to observe wild animals in wild habitat and the stories that follow range back and forth between domestic and wild animals. A couple focus on gorillas in a zoo. These ways of being animals differ from one another, but each teaches me, each beguiles my imagination in a similar way. For me, all the animals in the book are linked by the intensity of my experience of them. Fascinated by the way in which each animal exists fully in its own world, I am drawn by the animal into its world. Wild, domestic, zoo—or, for that matter, fictional or mythological—the form the animals in my life take is irrelevant. What matters to me is the connection with the power of nonhuman lives each form offers. It is the connection of spirit, of ancient memory, of beginnings in which all of us were spun out of the primordial mass. I believe in the community of our beginnings. This does not lessen the struggle to exist, or alter the chain of nature, but by making all of us equal in the beginning, it is the basis for connection.

ask now the beasts

the dog

༄

WE DROVE INTO the parking area at Hilltop, Arizona, in the early dark of late November. A dog with big white feet and a white chest—brilliantly visible in the black space—ran toward the truck, tail wagging, eager, as if he had been waiting for us. Bounding up as we opened the doors, he greeted us with joy. With expectation. He stayed close to the back door of the camper while we transferred things to the cab. He wanted food. He wanted to be friends.

When we woke in the early morning, he was curled against a tire of the car parked next to us. He rose when we did. Across the lot from us, three saddled horses stood tied by their reins to a long hitch rail. They had been there all night. One, coming loose as we went about the morning's chores, wandered across cracked pavement looking for grass that did not exist. Stepping on his reins, he pulled at the bit in his mouth. I untied his lead rope from its rag-end of a holder, led him back to the rail, and hitched him short. People arrived as the morning deepened, prepared themselves for hikes and horseback rides into the canyon—to the Supai village eight miles away or, two miles farther, to the campground below Havasu Falls. The dog greeted them all.

Packers, who had started the trek from the village to Hilltop early, pulled their pack trains up the last feet of the canyon wall, then tied their animals to the hitch rack, ready to load for the return trip. When the packer whom my husband, David, had engaged to carry our duffles arrived, we began our own hike.

I looked for the dog as we started down the canyon wall, but he was busy checking out who might offer him something. Disappointed at not saying goodbye, I had to recognize it was what I wanted. We had not fed him. I did not want him becoming attached to us only to feel—to be—abandoned. In the days we camped in the bottom of the canyon, I began to wonder about the selfishness in that. He, after all, needed food. We were incidental.

The long, steep switchbacking trail from Hilltop into the canyon is carved out of almost vertical limestone extending hundreds of feet down from the plateau. The limestone caps red sandstone enclosing red earth on the canyon floor almost 3,000 feet below. Packers passed us as we descended, some leading trains of fourteen or sixteen animals. Most goods coming into the village are packed in on horseback. Horses provide transportation in the village and the canyon. They are the way out of the canyon. Horses and one's own feet. Helicopters fly important guests, old people, and hurrying people in and out. They provide help in an emergency and bring in heavy equipment, like the all-terrain vehicles that haul garbage or carry luggage from the helipad to the hotel for the hurrying people. The village byways are dirt paths: soft, dusty, red-brown dirt, the earth of ancestors.

The helipad next to the café brings another dimension to the isolate life of this ancient people, a trade-off for retaining a semblance of the past. Skipping all middle roads, the Supai went directly from the silence of tardigrade eons to ear-splitting, gas-guzzling, high-speed technology. An odd juxtaposition when you have walked to the village from Hilltop, walked from one world into another through time measured in rock layers.

Dogs followed all the packers, happy to have work. The dog who had slept by the car tire had little exchange with the packers' dogs. He was interested in the non-Indian people who appeared. Non-Indians would give him food.

The canyon trail evolves into a dirt road into the village. A mile earlier, David had gone on ahead, so I approached the village alone. I heard the rush of a stream. After I crossed its blue water on a wooden bridge, the stream moved away from the trail. A man on horseback rode down to it from another direction, entering it to give his horse, and the horse he led, a drink. If he saw me, he did not acknowledge it. I came from a world he could not see, the way a dog does not see his reflection in a mirror. As I passed the first house, a man, bent under a heavy load of slender tree limbs, appeared on the road ahead of me. A second man rode past on a black horse. A dozen horses stood in the dry dust of a fenced yard. The houses grew closer together. A sign asked people to walk their horses. I entered the square formed by the café on one side of a large, open space, the store and post office on the other. A few old men lounged on the bench in front of the store.

Dogs wandered back and forth or lay on the sandy earth in front of the café. A notice on the community bulletin board announced the arrival of the veterinarian, who has been coming to the village for the past twenty-one years. Urging people to bring all their animals to the free clinic at the church, it suggested that everyone thank the vet for his years of volunteer service to the village.

One morning a dog came to our campsite. He lay down on the edge of it and waited. It was a routine for him. Find campers. Wait. Get food. I gave him none, for the same reason I had not fed the dog at Hilltop. I did not want him to become attached to us and be abandoned. After a while he stood and walked away. When he walked away, I felt the wrench in my heart you feel when you have made a mistake. He was different from the dog at Hilltop. This was just a day's work for him. Make the rounds. Get food. I went to look for him, to offer him cheese, the only food we had suitable for a dog. I found him at the edge of the single other inhabited campsite.

"Is that your dog?" I asked.

"He just comes and begs," they said. The dog looked at me without interest. He knew I had already not come through.

Buddhist monks wander the byways with their begging bowls. It is an honor to put food in the bowls. The dog had offered me the honor and I had turned from it out of my own selfish need not to say goodbye. I decided to feed the dog at Hilltop on our return the following day.

Stopping for a late lunch about three miles before the trail's end, we encountered the Hilltop dog following three students bound for the campground. We shared lunch with him and he stayed with us as we continued up the canyon and up the switchbacks on the canyon wall. He chased a chipmunk. He picked up bones along the way and proudly carried them along until something else attracted him. When we stopped to rest on the climb up the switchbacks, he rested too, laying his head on David's foot, or snuggling into my knee, as if we had been hiking together for a long time. He was happy to have people. At the top I gave him more cheese and a bowl of water. He lapped the water quickly and again, when I refilled the bowl. When I climbed into the truck, he came to the passenger side and put his front feet up on the cab floor, ready to go with us. I forced him away as gently as I could and closed the door, but he chased us as we drove out of the parking area, running as if his life depended on it, as if he were screaming at us not to leave without him. When he understood that he could neither catch us nor bring us back, he stopped. In the side-mirror reflection, I saw him watching the truck. He could not believe we were leaving.

We drove hours then, into the night. Hours away from him. We spent the following day driving across reservation land to the canyon of the Little Colorado. In all the miles, the dog running did not leave my heart. What did leave me were any scruples I had about taking a dog who may have belonged to someone. Yet, how could he belong to anyone when he was so clearly looking for people of his own? The next day, I drove five hours back to Hilltop to get him. At one o'clock on a weekday afternoon, there was not much activity in the parking area. Five saddled horses tethered to the hitch rack stood with their heads down, asleep in the afternoon heat. From the top of the trail I caught sight of two long pack trains winding their way down the steep cliff. I watched until they were absorbed into the huge red silence of the canyon. After that, nothing moved for a long time. The afternoon remained hot and absolutely still. I sat below the canyon rim in the shadow of the canyon wall surrounded by all the time that has ever existed, by the colors of the canyon, by silence. Three ravens appeared out of sky, circled above the canyon, disappeared into sky. The dog was not there. It had not occurred to me he would not be there. I expected another chance. Even knowing he might not be, I believed he would. Be waiting. Know I would come back for him. I climbed up the lip of the canyon to check all the corners of the parking area. An Indian walked from trash barrel to trash barrel, looking for something to eat, the man as hungry as the dog.

Through my binoculars I watched a packer move among his animals and the long trailers standing in a smaller parking area below this main one where I waited. He busied himself for a long time, never seeming to get the horses loaded. Two backpackers drove up, prepared their gear and started down into the canyon—a mother and daughter celebrating the mother's fiftieth birthday. A lone hiker emerged from the canyon. I asked if he had seen the dog. He had not.

Once the backpackers had all left the parking area I got into my car, uneasy about being in the parking area while Hungryman made his rounds. One of the five horses tied to the rail across from me lay down, attempted to roll. Stopped by his tether and the saddle, he lay quietly, the lead rope pulling his head into an awkward angle. Hungryman seemed not to notice him. When the packer working in the lower parking area led his saddle horse and several pack horses up to the main area, he shouted the horse to its feet. The packer wore a black cowboy hat. He and Hungryman walked together down the row of vehicles, checking each one. When they reached mine, they asked what I was doing.

"Waiting," I said.

"For who?"

"For friends."

A blue pickup drove into the area, let a man off by the trail. The man began the walk down without a glance anywhere. Someone who lives there. The dog could have followed someone down. Or any of the twenty-seven veterinarians convening in the canyon while we were there (their meeting coinciding with the regular vet's visit) might have taken him on their return—by helicopter—to Hilltop. Someone else could have taken him. He could be anywhere.

Hungryman slithered through the broken half of a window in the trailer that serves as the parking area office. In busier seasons, someone staffs the office. In any season, loads are left in front of the office by packers who have brought them up from the village, or by people who have arranged for packers to bring them down. The man came out of the window carrying a bag of cookies. He and Blackhat left in a small red car. All the horses remained tied to the hitch rail.

I sat in my car wondering how long I should wait. It was stupid to wait, stupid to expect the dog to be there. It was stupid not to have acted at once.

When the two men returned, Blackhat parked next to the hitch rail, leaving his car radio blaring to a country station while he and Hungryman began rigging pack saddles out of the riding saddles on the tethered horses. Hungryman was obviously the underling, the one who did the heavy work, Blackhat the boss. One horse balked, bucked, kicked. Hungryman yelled at it. A second car arrived, disgorged two more men who ducked under the hitch rail to help load. Blackhat leaned on the roof of the second car, talking to the woman at the steering wheel. A horse loaded earlier in the lower parking area lay down, then, under his load, could not get up again. Struggling to stand, he rose partway and fell back. Over and over. I watched the struggle, not believing none of the men saw it. Finally, reluctantly—frightened at how an Indian man would react to a white woman telling him something about his horses—I went to the car to interrupt Blackhat's conversation. A baby-faced twenty-five-year-old, he seemed confused by what I was telling him. He did not look toward the horse. As I wondered what to do next, he suddenly thanked me, left the car without further conversation with the woman and walked over to the horse. The woman drove away.

The four men were slow. They seemed clumsy, unconscious of the horses. While they were loading, a man on horseback leading a neatly loaded pack horse rode into the parking area from the road, spoke briefly with the four men, then continued into the canyon. It was already late in the afternoon. The four remaining could not reach the village before dark. At the rate they were moving, they would hardly be off the canyon wall before dark. I had watched a pack train being run two days earlier. I imagined that these horses, heavily loaded, would also be run.

I was exhausted watching the clumsiness of the packing; deeply disappointed at the absence of the dog. I had already imagined life with him, imagined the placement of his bed in the house and how happy he would be to have people of his own. He knew there was a different life. He knew we just drove away from him. I wondered if he would make it through the winter.

When the horses were almost entirely loaded, the balky horse rubbed hard against the horse next to him, sending that horse's load—in one of the plastic mail baskets the Supai use as panniers—crashing to the ground. The basket broke, spilling a sack of grain pellets that tore open and scattered in the dirt. "Fuck!" Hungryman yelled. He and the other two underlings scraped at the dirt, groveling for every pellet, as if they were gold dust. In a way, they are. Pellets are a necessity for feeding the Supai horses. Because grazing would soon make a desert of the canyon, all feed for the horses must be packed in. The three men poured the gathered pellets, dirt clinging to them, into the torn sack. The balky horse struggled to get free of his load. Thrashing, he fell to the ground, his neck oddly twisted. Blackhat—busy parking his car—finally appeared, untied the horse and kicked him up. A dog with Blackhat lunged and barked at the horse in his attempt to make it stand. The horse stood, lay down again, then quickly rose, as if to show his protest. The half-loaded horse next to him was repacked.

I had already decided that when the packers left, I would go. Without the dog. Before leaving the hotel in the morning, I had agreed with David that if the dog was at Hilltop, it was because he was supposed to be. If he was not, that, too, was supposed to be. My head ached. My body learned the expression *a heavy heart*. Heavy, heavy heart. I had agreed with David because I was so certain the dog would be there.

~⁓

I FAILED ANOTHER dog once. Schatzi.

It was a long time ago. I lived in a small cabin on a lake almost entirely surrounded by forest. At one end there were a few small houses. Schatzi lived in one of them, but she came to my cabin every day. She'd spend the day with me. At the end of the summer, I considered taking her back to the city with me. Stealing her. She belonged to people in one of the small houses. They had told me her name. When I returned the following summer and she did not come running to meet me, I went to the house where she lived.

"Where is Schatzi?" I asked.

"She died last winter. Froze to death," they said.

~⁓

THE HORSES, LOADED, were led to the trailhead. Blackhat threw stones at three who were loose, sending them down on their own. Hungryman rode, leading three. Blackhat rode and led three more.

I waited half an hour longer until, at the edge of night, I started the car and left, driving the long, empty road from Hilltop to the two-lane that passes through empty neon towns, driving the interstate to Grand Canyon National Park, driving through the pitch-black park, no one else on the road, no one else in the world. I drove without the dog. In his place, a huge sorrow, an emptiness like a hole in the earth. My headlights lit trees lining both sides of the road, ghost-green against a black sky, the black road, glaring yellow line down the center, bright reflectors at the edges, a beginning wind growing steadily stronger. The wind was bringing in cold. The car radio announced that temperatures would sink into the thirties during the night. The dog would begin to learn winter. It would be his first. He is a puppy.

I SHOULD HAVE waited. However long it took.

ace

❦

ACE AND I lead a line of twelve guests on horseback up Pelican Valley on a clear Yellowstone day, a day of crystal air. The water in Pelican Creek sparkles. Sandhill cranes ride the length of the sky, their ululating as primeval as the place. Scattered across the valley, small groups of buffalo graze tall, yellowing grass, the grass barely moving in the calm noon.

Our trail follows the edge between meadow and forest. Grass on both sides of the trail is almost as high as Ace's chest. This is familiar territory to him and he walks comfortably, knowing we will come to camp with good pasture before many more miles have elapsed. The three mules behind us—Buck, Sis, and Festus—are just as much at home. All the horses are. I watch the forest for movement—a grizzly bear, a wolf, a deer. Twice in the past, when a deer appeared out of nowhere as we rode through forest, Ace reared and bolted, reacting to the sudden appearance of a creature erupting into his vision. Twice I had dropped the rope to the mules so that I could freely turn him and calm him and get him back into his place in line. Dropping the rope is not ideal, because the mules can wander off, but it beats getting the rope wrapped around something—Ace's leg or my arm or any number of other things—in the mercurial movements of the horse and my own focused attention on getting the situation settled.

Those moments apart, Ace is a good lead horse. He is strong and agile and he knows the Yellowstone trails as intimately as I know the rooms in my house. But horses are prey animals. In their genes, they are always wary. Unexpected things scare them. So I have learned to watch for those things, to see them first, before Ace does.

That's how it is in my mind—until this trip. A grizzly appears near the trail and I am not the first to see it. I do not even suspect its presence until Ace simply stops in his tracks, ears up, forward, his whole body alert, like a dog on point. Fifty feet ahead of us, a row of grass moves like a wave from the meadow up to the trail. A two-year-old grizzly emerges from it, crosses the path, and continues toward the forest. He crosses the path without looking at us, as if we were nothing on his morning errands. For an instant, I can see his back as he moves through the grass. I think he might circle back to the trail. I think there might be a Mama Bear somewhere who will follow him through the high grass and across the path. Bears usually stay with their mothers for two years, before setting off on their own. When Ace stops and I hold up my hand, the riders behind me take out binoculars and cameras, but the bear disappears in the grass, so all any of us can see is a line of grass moving until a wind comes up and all the meadow grass moves. I do not see him enter the forest, but when no sow appears, and he does not reappear in a reasonable time, we ride on, although I suggest to the outfitter that perhaps he would like to ride lead for a while.

I am quickly sorry about this momentary lapse into my basic cowardice, because I like it when Ace and I lead. I like the feeling that only the two of us—and, of course, my mules—are out there, that we are in wild country on our own and that, between us, we can deal with anything. The grandness of companionship Ace offers me gives me courage. As if the two of us could do anything. All good trail horses offer this. (Other horses do, too, but I don't have experience with hunters and jumpers or other, more civilized horse events.) This companionship with the horse is why a backcountry pack trip is so extraordinary for anyone who gets as involved with the horse she or he rides as with the landscape. You share an adventure. Shared *experience*—felt in the rider the same way the horse feels every movement of the rider's body, every emotion, every thought in the rider's mind, every waft of air and moment of sun—seems to me deeper than shared words. The horse may or may not understand the word *whoa*, but he will certainly react to the way you sit. Words used to translate an experience make the experience secondhand, a superficial event. But if things are superficial between you and your horse, at least one of you is in trouble. The beauty of a horseback trip is that whatever happens to one of you happens to you both.

And there is only what happens. What happens is always in the present moment. The miracle of relationship with a horse, a dog, any animal is the necessity to be present *this* moment. (Same thing with a person, but it's harder to do. People like to hitch themselves to words. Animals attend to what exists.) What Ace and I share is in each moment we share. Wildflower meadows and noon sun; cool streams on a hot day; cold, wet, long rides; cloudbursts; dawn; and all forty-five billion stars of all forty-five billion universes. We have negotiated fast, high streams and eased the mules safely around tight places. We have been tired together, grateful for trail's end. We have shared apples and time and a lot of miles. I know how his muscles and his strength and his awareness feel without a saddle or with. He knows how I ride and what I expect and how I love him. He knows there are places that scare me, and that he does not scare me. I know he can handle the places that scare me. He knows I can handle him. We work well together.

my dog

❧

I SKIED PAST Old Faithful Lodge, its huge, dark, turreted, closed-up presence like the gothic silence of abandoned time. What seems glorious solitude to me in uninterrupted nature becomes great loneliness in a building closed against the season. In its proximity, winter lies so deeply in itself, complete, absolute, without memory of other seasons.

There had been many people at breakfast in the Snow Lodge, but there was no one anywhere around me now. I passed the Old Faithful Lodge, grateful to be away from it, crossed a small bridge, and headed up the ski trail toward Lone Star Geyser. Fresh snow, a sparkling morning, the Firehole River flowing cold-gray beside me. The trees on the slope bounding the trail on my right were heavy with snow. Snow topped boulders in the river on my left. Elk tracks crossed and recrossed the ski track, leaving huge holes in it. You can't get mad at an elk for stepping in the ski track, I thought. It was a brilliant morning, with nothing but snow and river and trees, elk tracks and sky in sight. The trail was level, easy, utterly beautiful. The sun moved. The river moved. I moved. In a morning of no wind, the trees did not move.

There is a timelessness in extreme beauty. The present does not disappear. Now becomes eternal. Once David said to me, "Let's do now forever." It is what I was doing, skiing along the Firehole. I did not rush. A short way before Lone Star Geyser, I approached a rise in the trail. On my left, the river had been replaced by a long, downhill slope to a vast snow meadow. A man and a woman stood on the rise, staring at me. Nothing improves one's skiing like people watching. Those two looked like great skiers. They looked as though they ran five miles every morning before breakfast.

I straightened up. I skied better. My glide became longer, my arms reached further forward. I became stronger, taller.

"Is that your dog?" the man asked me.

I thought perhaps there was an elk somewhere behind me and the man was joking about the elk that had been postholing the trail. There could not be a dog here. Dogs are not allowed on trails in the park. I turned to look behind me. A coyote stood at the end of my ski. If I reached back, I could touch him.

I turned back to the couple. "No," I said, "That's not my dog."

It seemed to take me a long time to register what was happening. I turned, again, to look at the coyote, really looking at him this time, taking in a well-fed, healthy animal with a thick, shiny coat and eyes that returned my look. We each saw that the other was not frightened. In looking at him, I forgot one is not supposed to look into the eyes of a wild animal. I looked into the eyes of my dog. The coyote returned my look, then turned and trotted off down the slope on my left. I watched him go the whole long way down to the meadow until he disappeared behind some distant trees.

"That's not my dog," I said to the couple again.

"He was following right behind you the whole way," the man said.

The trail behind me came out of a curve several hundred yards away. Beyond that, it was not possible to see from where the couple and I stood.

"He was as close to you as when you stopped," the man said.

I always think I am aware in wild country. I think my senses are alert to everything around me. Even so, I also look behind me quite frequently (in case a lion or a bear has appeared on the trail). Or I thought I did. It seems I do not do that on skis. Skis are so emphatically impelled forward that they do not promote looking around as hiking does. Apparently, my senses are not as keen as I imagine, either, although snow muffles the sounds of other seasons. It changes the aura of things. Should I not develop awarenesses in concert with the season? Perhaps I've been away from serious winter too long. Perhaps I've lost the necessity to be intimate with every season. Perhaps I would have felt malevolence or fear or hunger, where I did not notice ease. Had I sensed the coyote was there and turned to see him, he would have gone sooner, would have made less use of the packing my skis did on the trail. The guy was a hitchhiker, and I gave him a ride.

in the course of things

※

THE CLIFF CROWNS the tree-covered mountain like a castle. High vertical rock towering 2,000 feet above the dirt road that offers approach to it, it is an eyrie fit for gods. Or falcons.

The narrow dirt road follows a creek running cold and dark, riffling, rippling, arching, and sparkling the miles of its run down from the mountains into the river in the main canyon. But on the castled mountain, there is no water. There are trees and rock, grasses, shrubbery, wildflowers, mule deer, lions, mice, martens, birds. But no water. From every view point on the mountain you can see water—teasing, rushing, all those feet below.

For a falcon, the flight from the cliff to the creek is no big deal. This is one of those places on earth where a falcon has all it needs— a high rock cliff safe from predators on the ground, good hunting, nearby water. The falcon's eye is powerful enough to see, from the cliff, all that is happening on the creek.

The area was one used by The Peregrine Fund for its restoration of the once almost-extinct peregrine falcon to the wild. (Peregrines were removed from the endangered species list in 1999, after the most comprehensive effort to restore wild populations of an endangered species ever accomplished.) Reintroduction sites, like this one, existed across the country. They made use of rock cliffs, towers constructed where the situation was ideal except for the lack of a suitable cliff, in cities. Cities being, after all, just human-made cliffs, the sheer sides of their high buildings offering the same kind of protection a peregrine falcon seeks in the wild. Some people say there are unbridgeable differences between cities and wilderness, but some people find unbridgeable differences in everything.

Environments that can support peregrines have a connection to one another, and if we cannot see the wildness for the civilization, it is only our loss. Wildness doesn't care. Wildness can take over at any moment. And it will. If we succeed in destroying life on this planet, it is wildness that will, in time, come back. Not us. The next time around, life will probably try some form that works better.

Once, driving down the West Side Highway when I still lived in New York City, I saw a peregrine perched on a guardrail post at about 100th Street. The falcon sat there, watching, its body perfectly still, its eyes watching. I couldn't stop on the highway. I had to drive on past, as if passing a peregrine on the West Side Highway were ordinary, something you'd do any day. At first I thought I had invented the peregrine. Later, I remembered reading about a nesting pair under the George Washington Bridge. The George Washington Bridge connects New York to New Jersey and the Rocky Mountains. For a number of years, I had been driving up the highway from my apartment on the Upper West Side, across the bridge, then straight west to Wyoming or Montana. The bridge was a direct link between my house and the Rocky Mountains.

After I moved permanently to Montana, I went to work for The Peregrine Fund as a hack-site attendant, one of two people assigned to each peregrine release site in the country, to feed, observe, track, and generally watch out for the young peregrines hatched in the laboratory, and hacked to the wild. Hacking is a falconer's term for the process that allows for the natural physical conditioning of birds of prey taken from the nest before they can fly. The falconer places young birds on some conspicuous structure (The Peregrine Fund used a wooden box that became the birds' home until they were old enough to begin flying) and provides them with food. Once the birds start flying, they still return daily to the site for food. As they learn to hunt and begin making their own kills, they spend more and more time away from the hack site. At this point, a falconer retraps his birds, taming them to be trained for sport. The Peregrine Fund, on the other hand, simply hoped their birds had learned enough to survive in the wild. Eighty percent of them did not survive.

Three days before I was to begin my summer as an attendant, I had a climbing accident that resulted in my right arm requiring six stitches and an unstitchable hole in my right leg below my knee. I could put little pressure on my leg and could hardly use my arm. I am right-handed. I had to drive in second gear because my left arm could not reach far enough to push the shift into any higher gear. The job required a daily climb of about sixty feet down to the ledge where the young peregrines were kept in their hack box, as well as tending to camp chores.

Why had I done this just before the beginning? I had been looking forward to this time on the mountain for months. Had I deliberately sabotaged it? Was I somehow afraid of it? I believe there are no accidents. Coincidence does not exist. Things that seem random are merely unfathomable. Cancelling at this last minute seemed irresponsible, but I knew I could not climb. I phoned The Peregrine Fund to let them know what had happened.

"Can you get up to camp?" the director asked me.

"Yes," I answered.

"Your partner can take care of the climbing." he said.

His voice was calming, reassuring. It all seemed possible, yet I was devastated. My partner would be up there with the birds while I would be in camp, watching through my spotting scope.

I arrived at the meeting spot on time, Thursday at noon. One of two biologists who would help us set up camp arrived soon after. The other, coming from Boise, Idaho, with my partner and our falcons, arrived two hours late. They had been on the road since one in the morning. My partner, Stefania, looked dazed and disheveled from the long trip. When she lifted her backpack onto her back for the first haul up to camp, the sleeping bag, awkwardly tied at the bottom, dangled half off the pack. The backpack itself was army surplus. This woman would take care of the climbing?

Leaving our backpacks at the campsite, we followed the biologists who carried four baby falcons in two large square cardboard cartons marked "Hertz Rent-All" up the cliff where the hack box sat on a narrow ledge, tethered to the ledge by cable nailed into the rock back behind the box. There was just room at the sides of the box and behind it for a person to stand. The biologists showed Stefania, who had never climbed before, how to use her climbing harness and how to tie into the belay set up around a sturdy tree at the top of the climb. Then all three downclimbed the cliff that led to the ledge and hiked across the ledge to prepare the hack box. I watched them go down and across and work at the box, wretched because I had allowed myself to be left out. They had taken one carton of falcons with them. While they were occupied at the hack box, I peeked through one of the airholes in the remaining carton and came eye to eye with a falcon. I was not supposed to do this, not supposed to disturb the baby birds in any way, disturb them any more than they had already been disturbed by being taken from the only place they had ever known, put into a box, and driven some four hundred miles through the night to be carried up 2,000 feet and a mile and a half of mountain. I knew I wasn't supposed to.

At the peephole, a great, round, dark, fierce eye drew my own eye in.

When the hack box was ready, the biologists returned for the remaining falcons. At the box again, the three of them watched as the falcons settled into their new home. It seemed a long time that I watched the biologists and Stefania observing the birds. When the biologists felt sure everything was in order, the three walked back across the ledge and climbed up the wall. We packed the climbing gear into a stuff bag, tied it to the tree where it would stay for the duration, and hiked back down to camp. The hot sky clouded over. It was almost seven when we reached camp.

We still had a few loads waiting to be carried up to camp, and camp to be set up. One of the biologists, the only male among us, began hauling eighty-pound containers of water the thousand-foot, three-quarter-mile climb from the road to camp. There was no water at the campsite. Every drop we used had to be carried up. I would have to keep my wounds clean without water. What we had, needed for drinking and cooking, was too precious for that. Rain began as we put up the tent. Hurrying, we threw our gear into it, then headed back to the road for the final load. It was late now and growing dark. The biologists left. Alone, our last ascent to camp would be in darkness.

Stefania, who I had already seen was very strong, and a faster walker than I even when my leg was all right, was afraid there would be bears in the dark. I led the way, grateful for the night, for the end of this day. Observer. My usual role. It is why I am a writer. But I am an actor as well, and on this day I was out of the essential action. I felt displaced.

I walked without using my flashlight, feeling the path more than seeing it. The rain stopped. The night cleared. Starlight reflected off white stones. Earth and sky were the same. My feet were on earth, my head in sky. I liked walking in the night. Besides, I knew there were no bears. Confiding my one anxiety about this site to a landscape architect I knew who worked for the national forest where the site was located, I had said, "The only thing I'm worried about is bears."

"There ain't no fuckin' bears up there," she reassured me.

At camp we got the stove going, ate a late dinner, and had a chance, finally, to meet one another. Stefania had been hired the day before. When The Peregrine Fund had told me that my partner could take care of the climbing, I actually had no partner. My original partner had called them the day before I called, to say she'd taken a job training horses in Colorado. The director had sounded so calm. He must have been frantic, but he also must have had faith this would work out. Climber, falconer, he had spent a lifetime being patient.

I had hardly thought about my partner beforehand. You would think that someone about to spend eight weeks living in a tent with another person—being together more or less twenty-four hours a day—might spend a little time wondering about that person. It is, after all, the kind of time that could cement a love affair or a friendship forever, or end either one in a short time. Taking on that kind of time with a stranger is a bit like answering an ad for a mail-order bride, except this one had fewer outs.

But I had only thought about the falcons. After the accident, I had just hoped my partner would be competent, but I also worried that terrific competence would make me extraneous. I did not want to be extraneous. I wished I were doing this alone. I wished I had not injured myself.

Stefania was a volunteer at the World Center for Birds of Prey in Boise—Peregrine Fund headquarters—and a recent graduate with a major in zoology. When my erstwhile partner called to say she'd taken another job, and I called to say I couldn't climb, The Peregrine Fund asked Stefania if she was free to take this on. They asked her late in the afternoon of the day before we were to open the site. She had a job commitment for that evening, so it was eleven at night before she began getting her gear together. Not that she had much: She had backpacked one weekend in her life. Somehow, she managed to borrow a pack and sleeping bag, throw together a few clothes, and take off at one in the morning with the biologist who was bringing the birds. She had slept a little in the truck, but not much.

She hauled gear up from the vehicles parked on the road below. She climbed easily down to the hack box. She climbed a tree near camp to tie the rope from which we would suspend our food coolers to keep them out of reach of critters—ground squirrels as much as bears. She dug the latrine. She helped me get the tent up and arrange a tarp to shelter our kitchen. I apologized that I could do so little, but she handled everything with grace. She asked how to do the things she had never done, then did them simply, without making me feel how little I could actually do. She was physically strong and incredibly gentle in her relation to me, to all that was around us, work and birds and earth and heaven.

She was twenty years younger than I, and we would become friends.

～

FOR THE FIRST couple of mornings, we hiked up to the cliff together. Then she climbed down to leave the quail we had brought for the falcons to eat, watched the falcons through peepholes in the box, and climbed back up while I sat on top of the cliff, pistol in hand—to shoot blanks at any passing eagles and scare them out of the territory before they got the idea there were young peregrines here to harass. We did not want them around once the peregrines were out of the box. On the rocks above the cliff, watching the sky, I felt sick with longing. I knew I had to climb.

The doctor had told me the one thing I must guard against was banging either wound, or I risked serious infection, no trifle under field conditions. But a friend, Bob, a strong man, was coming to visit on

Saturday. I decided to go down to the box while he was there. If I had problems at all with the climb, he was strong enough to simply haul me up again.

My knees felt shaky as I stepped into my climbing harness. Bob stood at the top of the cliff, waiting for me to start. I started slowly, reaching with my foot down the narrow wall for the little knob that would allow me a beginning. I was frightened, but I had started. The knob was solid, easy. And the next, and the next. It was not hard. On the rock I saw it was not hard: It was a vertical staircase. When I looked up I could see Bob standing calmly at the top, Stefania behind him. I was still nervous, but it was easier now, having started, than it had been standing on top, thinking about it. Doing a thing is easier than not doing it.

I could see Bob leaning over the edge until I reached the bottom, where my view of him was cut off by the wall itself. But then I did not need to see him anymore. I had done it. I had only to walk across the ledge to the birds. I untied and made my way to the hack box. Here, now, for the reason I had come, I was no longer separate. I lifted the flap on one of the peepholes, keeping my finger over the hole until my eye covered it so that, for the birds, the dark wall would remain uninterrupted.

From the screened front of the box set on the cliff's edge, the peregrines' view was of sky, of forest below the sky, forest falling away to the creek, of forest and mountains beyond the creek reaching up to sky again. Everything there was, was defined by sky.

Four peregrines stood there looking out at swallows and insects flitting past, at bits of down from their own coats that floated out on the light, bright sky. Babies. Grave, funny birds with down sprouting out from under their wings and sticking through their breast feathers. I could already see how different each was from the others. We had decided against naming them because, in the wild, peregrines do not have names, and because names could engender attachment on our part, attachment in some more personal way than the kind of universal attachment to all of life. We were there to observe and record, not to love. But it was still necessary for us to identify them individually. We decided to refer to them by the color of the leg bands The Peregrine Fund had attached to their right legs to identify them. On their left legs they wore black federal bands with a number given each by the U.S. Department of Fish & Wildlife. The result was that the words *blue, yellow, red,* and *green* became as much names for us as *David* or *Chloe.*

The peregrines watched everything that passed and took considerable note of each other's movement. They preened, spread their wings, moved about the box, jumped on and off the two rock perches on the box floor. Each bird was different from the others, but one was more different. Blue. Boldest, most regal, he was the most active of the four. He spread his wings with such air of majesty that you knew you were in the presence of no ordinary bird. He jumped from one rock perch to the other, jumped at the bars, at the box door. He jumped on the other peregrines. The box seemed too small for him. He was so eager for the world. Blue was beautiful. They were all beautiful, but Blue was the most beautiful. Wild, wild and beautiful.

When the peregrines were ready to fledge, eight days after they arrived, the biologist returned to help with their release from the box. The peregrines were taken from the box individually, outfitted with tiny radio transmitters tuned to individual frequencies, then returned to the box. Stefania and I learned each bird's frequency so that we could track them separately on the telemetry receiver left with us. Once these preliminaries were completed, the front was removed from the box and the peregrines were free to leave it on their own timing. All four exited quickly. Blue immediately jumped to the top of the box to check out the world. The others followed. He was the second to fly, but he flew as if he understood flight from the moment of birth. The other falcons, like most falcons, made short flights in the beginning, practice flights, learning what flight is, how to take off and to land, their practice strengthening the muscles needed for longer forays. Blue didn't bother with all that. He took off in a beeline for the ridge to the east, flew behind it, and was gone.

He was really gone. He did not come back that day to eat, or the next, or the next. We had been told a young falcon could survive four days without food. That is, if it did not encounter an owl or a golden eagle, or land on the forest floor from which it might have a hard time launching itself skyward again. On the forest floor, a young falcon is easy prey for foxes or lynx, coyotes, badgers. In the air, it can be taken down by other raptors. It is a favorite food of owls. More than once has a young falcon's radio transmitter been found lying at the foot of an owl's tree, tangled among a few cleaned bones. Just out of the box, the falcon doesn't know how to hunt, does not have the skill to outmaneuver a predator in flight, has no technique for evasion, or the security of that tremendous power into which it will grow. The first weeks for a young falcon are treacherous ones.

We searched for Blue with the telemetry, picking up his signal in one direction and, almost immediately, in the opposite direction. It came weakly from what seemed great distances, or it bounced along ridges, reflecting back from them. We hiked miles trying to pick up a clear direction, imagining—against our wills—that the weak signal came from the transmitter lying at the foot of some owl's tree. By the third day we were pretending calmness. By the fourth, we believed he must be dead. He was a baby. What skill could he have to survive so long on his own?

I searched the sky for him and he did not return. In spite of the other three in the sky, the sky seemed empty to me. As empty as the house seems, or the town, when one's lover is absent. No, *lover* is the wrong word. Beloved. The one who makes the world exist on that plane where everything is seen, felt, experienced in full clarity of its power, its grace, its unutterable beauty, its hope, and its amazing life. Some magic, glorious, soaring moment had disappeared from me. The more I mourned his loss, the more he became, for me, mine. I continued to watch the others, to note their every action in my notebook. I was fascinated by them, but I felt empty. My peregrine was gone . . .

~

IN THE LATE afternoon of the fifth day, Stefania and I were both sitting at our scopes in the meadow. It had been a hot day. The birds had spent the heat of the afternoon roosting in cool niches on the wall. Now, with the sun lower, they erupted into the sky. Watching them shoot up from the wall, I suddenly realized there were four peregrines in the sky.

Blue had come back. Blue was alive. My beautiful bird was alive. He had gone far and come back and he was alive. He flew with the others, the four of them filling the sky with the glory of falcons and the miracle of return. Blue had come back.

～つ

OUR DAYS SETTLED into routine. We alternated mornings to climb up to the box and leave the day's allotment of quail, each of us making the 1,000-foot, three-quarter-mile climb to the cliffs alone, tying in, climbing down. I was nervous at first, but, as the days went on, I grew calmer, realizing that I knew what I was doing and needed only to be willing to trust that I knew. I relished that morning time. I felt as if the peregrines were mine alone. I could climb. I was strong. I was healthy. I was healing.

I was happier than I had ever been. I began to see my fall as a gift, a chance to see what healing is. Why, after all, did nothing break when I landed so hard, and in so complicated a way, on rock? How was it that I was able to walk away from the fall, to get to the hack site on time? I had received two difficult, serious wounds, but they were wounds that would heal, that I could watch healing. They required an hour's attention daily, but they were healing. Healing takes time and leaves scars, but it makes one whole. The gift I was given was the chance to see how the process works. I do not know it if is possible to understand more by watching the process, but it is possible to see the process happen; to feel the relief and joy of healing; the good luck of it; to feel how resilient one is after all, how whole one can become.

It happens in its own time. It is in the course of things.

❧

So is the sunrise and the day and the sunset, the easy comfort Stefania and I developed with one another. We found a balance no different from the balance of meadow grass and forest, and the glorious flight of peregrines erupting into the sky, soaring, diving, flipping over, turning so that the sun glints off their breasts, chasing one another and tumbling through the sky like puppies on the ground, falling free to rise again on some splendid moment of air.

How near, how intimate the sky becomes.

❧

Toward the end of August, the air smelled of autumn. It happened overnight. The mornings became cool and I built fires to warm us during breakfast, then sat over coffee in front of the fire, watching the cliff. The birds were learning to hunt, although it was still a game for them. We continued setting out quail, but cut back to every other day shortly before closing the site in September. The peregrines would leave soon. Picking up their rightful instinct, they would join in with other passing raptors and be gone.

blue

❧

SEVERAL YEARS AFTER Rex, my wirehaired terrier, died and a year after my marriage ended, I moved from New York to Montana. Rex was part of my life for sixteen years; that husband, for eighteen. Neither of us wanted to leave the dog.

After Rex, I did not want—ever—to go through another dog's death. You know that dogs die. You hope your dog dies before you do so that it never has to live without you. You pray your dog will die on its own to spare you making the decision that it is time. That's what our family dog, a German short-haired pointer, did while I was away at college. One morning, after a long lifetime with us, she asked my father to let her out and, outside, she died. She was ten weeks old when my father bought her for fifteen dollars. My brother and I grew up with her. She watched over us and played with us and guarded our bicycles when we rode them to school. According to my father, there was never a bird dog as good. Everyone my father ever hunted with wanted to buy her, but she was not for sale. Her name was Rex. Years later, when my brother got a miniature dachshund, he named it Rex. When I got my wirehair, I named him Rex. For us both, it was the only *real* name for a dog.

Helping our animals go when it is time, rather than insisting they hang on beyond time, is more humane than what we demand of people. We are reluctant to proffer the same humanity to people, forcing them to live when what they want is help out of life. Yet, even when helping those we love is possible for us, we pray they will die on their own and save us the act. As we do with animals we love. We are not good at decisions about death. We think God should take care of it. We forget we are the agents of God, God ourselves. My mother asked for help and I could not help her, although in the medications I was given to ease her last night, perhaps I sped it up. I never asked. I think I could not handle knowing. I do not want to call time for anyone else. Not my mother. Not my dog. I have now had ample opportunity to see that, although my philosophy dictates otherwise, my instincts may converge on the idea of life at any cost. As long as it is not *my* life. I do not want *my* life unnecessarily prolonged to suit someone else's image of what life is. Or because making that decision is too hard.

How, in the name of love, do you allow a loved one to linger in suffering that is only ended by the grace of death? How do you allow that friend to linger in life that is not life but some hanging-on of the body's insistence on breath when breath is no longer to the point?

Rex could no longer stand by himself. Eating and drinking were of no interest. He lay on his bed no longer remembering life, his eyes showing that this was not life, his eyes asking for change. I phoned my mother to ask her thoughts. "You have no choice," she said. My mother loved all animals. She offered no opinion lightly. I knew my mother's wisdom. I disagreed entirely. I waited another day, praying he would die on his own. Either that, or become young again. And then there was no choice. We carried him to the vet, who laid him on the cold table. We said good-bye to him as the vet injected him with death. The line between life and death is so slim as to seem irrelevant. One instant there is life, the next, death. The body alive is no longer alive. It is an incomprehensible event.

And then you leave your beloved dog where he lies and go outside. We went to Zabar's and had coffee. We didn't know what else to do.

Although life with a dog seemed the natural way to live, I told my husband I would never go through another dog's death.

~

SHORTLY BEFORE MOVING to Montana, I visited a friend to see the Wheaten terrier puppy he had just gotten for his children. He had looked all over the east for a Wheaten, he told me, before finding one in Maryland. "They're hard to find," he said.

Falling in immediate love with the dog, I decided that if ever I were to get another dog—which, of course, I would not—it would be a Wheaten. I thought about it when I got to Montana, figuring that any dog as chic and hard to find as a Wheaten would not exist in Montana. Since it was the only dog I would consider, I was safe from ever having to get another dog.

Every time we spoke on the phone during my first five years in Montana, my father said, "I think you should get a dog." One afternoon,

I walked past a yard where a dog ran to the fence to see me. He looked like a Wheaten. I mentioned this to a friend, who insisted I return to the house to ask. "I'll go with you," he offered, virtually pulling me to the door.

"I passed your yard earlier," I said to the woman who came to the door. "I saw a dog that looked like a Wheaten."

"Oh, yes!" the woman said. "Come in."

We spent an hour there. Knowing I did not want a dog, I left with the breeder's phone number in my pocket. She turned out to be one of several Wheaten breeders in Montana at the time. I called her. She said she expected a litter in the spring.

"Oh, but I can't have a spring puppy because I spend all summer in the mountains," I said, relieved the matter was settled. "I can't take that young a puppy on a long backpack."

"No," the breeder agreed. "But if I ever have a fall litter, I'll let you know."

Several months later she sent me a note. A litter was due in October. I called her again. "I only want a male," I said, figuring I still had a fifty-fifty chance of not getting a dog.

Near the end of October, a second note arrived. "There are two puppies," she wrote, "both males."

When I phoned, she told me one was spoken for. "I want the other one," I said.

She asked me his name. "Blue," I said.

Blue. Like Rex, a real dog's name. Old Blue. "I have a dog, and his name is Blue. Betcha five dollars he's a good dog, too . . ." For hill people in the old South, where hunting was a subsistence way of life, a good hound dog who could help them track and catch food was worth his weight in gold. Country folk wrote songs of praise in the dog's honor, like the one about the good dog Blue, and mourned his death with song.

And then there was the peregrine, Blue, most magnificent of the four in my care. Grander than all the world's peregrines. I wanted to honor him, but I also *knew* my dog would be his equal, a *real* dog, one who hiked Montana's wildest country, climbed its highest mountains, skied with me all winter; one who lay at my feet when I worked or read; one who understood the responsibility of being a *dog*. An ultimate Wheaten.

When he was ten weeks old, I drove about four hours to Huson, Montana, to pick him up. He looked like a little rag mop with a truffle nose. I sent his photo to my parents. My father called. "I told you to get a dog, not a mop," he said.

"You're brave for taking on a terrier by yourself," the vet said. When Blue was twelve weeks old, I asked the vet if he was too young to take skiing. "Good idea," the vet said. "Ski about a mile and you'll wear him out so you can get some work done."

We skied about five miles because his energy never flagged. Every once in a while, between the uphill and downhill ski tracks, he got high-centered—stuck on snow that held him up by his belly but didn't allow his legs to touch anything solid. I stopped, picked him up, replaced him in my track. He weighed so little, he hardly made a dent in the track. By the time we returned to the car, I was exhausted; he was raring to go. Perhaps the vet was right about rearing a terrier on one's own.

We backpacked and hiked and climbed mountains. We traveled a great deal. For Blue's entire life, people stopped me—on the street, or in the mountains, everywhere I went—and said, "Is *that* a Wheaten?" It was always the same phrase, same emphasis, except for a woman walking toward us on a crowded promenade in a Tallahassee, Florida, park. We were making several rounds of the promenade for our evening walk. She was doing the same thing, without a dog. As she approached us, looking only at Blue, she said, "You look just like a movie star." Once we visited an editor of mine in Boulder, Colorado. I had never been there and she was showing me town. A man came up to me and said, "Where did you *get* him!? They're harder to get than dope!"

People who love dogs are interested in every dog they pass. But the reaction to a Wheaten is on another plane. Maybe Wheaten breeders are less guilty of overbreeding than breeders of some other dogs. Maybe there is less of the abuse perpetrated by American Kennel Club standards for the show ring that Mark Derr describes in his book *Dog's Best Friend.* Maybe that is why Wheatens are harder to get than dope. They are more interesting than addiction.

SUMMERS, WHEN I worked in Yellowstone, Blue spent much of the time with his friend, Murphy, a Wheaten three years his junior who lives in Billings. Murphy's people—Kathy and Tom—took the two of them hiking and backpacking. Together, Blue and Murphy worked out serious rock techniques for chasing marmots. One barked at the den entrance to flush the marmot out; the other stayed on the rocks above, where he could not be seen by the emerging marmot, to chase the marmot back into a rocky den. They alternated jobs, climbing higher and higher up the talus slope. In this way, many Montana marmots were seriously exercised, while the two dogs, herders by nature, continually increased their rock climbing technique. On walks in town, two well-matched Wheatens drew a great deal of attention. Kathy and Tom were quite pleased that everyone thought they had two Wheatens. When Murphy came to Bozeman to spend time with Blue, I felt the same way.

Like all terriers, Blue was independent. It is why I have developed a passion for terriers. If a terrier does not obey, it is not because he does not understand, but because he has decided either the command is silly or there is something else more important. You can see the dog making a decision. He does not do this lightly. I can only admire the spirit of someone who does not do as he is told because it makes no sense to him, who cares to think for himself. Blue always did the correct thing, even if it was not the correct thing as *I* saw it.

Chasing a ball seemed ridiculous to him. Your person throws a ball and you run to pick it up and bring it back and the whole thing is repeated. Anybody can do that. But to *imagine* the ball . . . to run as far as you imagine the ball has been thrown, to gauge the thrower's arm, the thrower's power, to see the distance the imagination runs, then chase it with all your power and speed, to retrieve *imagination* from the throw and return with it to the thrower . . . now *that* makes sense. It is an act of art, and Blue was an artist, someone who could visualize what did not yet exist, put his heart into creating it, retrieve what was in his mind, believe it could happen again and again, over and over for a lifetime.

～つ

THAT WAS MY dog. . . .

～つ

WHEN A FRIEND took Blue for a walk, he did not miss me. The image
I had of a dog lying at my feet belonged to another kind of dog. Not
Blue. At the same time I occasionally dreamed of a dog completely
loyal to me, I rejoiced in his willingness to make a life of his own. If
someone else was willing to play, he was perfectly content to lie at that
person's feet when the play was done. Not that he was unaware of me.
He just understood that slavish connection to one person was as illog-
ical as it was not to love. "I'm always true to you, darling, in my fash-
ion . . ." might have been his song.

He *knew* everyone in the world was his friend. Many people knew
him who did not know me. Sometimes when friends walked him, he
met people on his own. If they saw me with him later, they carried
on their relationship with him as if I were incidental. I liked that he
had his own life but chose to be with me. He was my best friend. I
think, for all his sociability, he would have said that I was his.

After the first twelve years of his life in Montana, Blue moved to
New Mexico with me when I left to marry David. I know he missed
the beautiful clear Montana creeks he so loved to run in (even though
he must be the only dog in the world who could not swim), and the
mountain trails he hiked and backpacked with such joy. In New
Mexico, we hiked the nearby trails at the bottom of Sandia Mountain, but they are desert trails, without creeks, without much shade,

desert-hot in summer. The Rio Grande Bosque near our house was shady and pleasant, but the river itself is mostly mud. (*Bosque* means "woods" in Spanish, a language long predating English in New Mexico.) The Bosque was fine for a morning walk, but it was not the Montana wilderness.

And yet, Blue was old by the time we came to New Mexico. Twelve years is the usual lifetime for a Wheaten. He had problems with his back from too many years of jumping up and down rocks, of leaping through meadows—bounding up and up and up to see over the high grasses, or from the pure joy of jumping—of leaping high into the air to catch the snow he liked kicked skyward for him. He no longer always heard my voice. Perhaps the Bosque came at the right time. Perhaps the earth works out our timing so that we do not interpret change as loss.

In his last weeks, it became difficult for him to stand up or lie down, although he was always able to summon the strength and energy to chase Lion, the cat who had come with us from Montana but had never before lived in the house. Blue chased Lion whenever he saw him. David thought Lion deliberately appeared in front of Blue as therapy, to rouse him into life. A friend suggested Blue was intent on living because he was not about to have a *cat* take his place. This idea he had that cats were out of the question was really his only flaw.

There came an evening when he could not get up, when he could not stand even when I held him. He looked at me then with so much hurt in his eyes. "You don't have to do this anymore," I said to him, and lay next to him all night. I prayed he would fall asleep and sleep and sleep forever. He did not sleep. Lion came into the room and Blue did not see him. In the morning I called the vet. He said he would come to the house at the end of the day. I lay next to Blue all day. I held him when the vet injected death. I brushed him then and laid him on his bed in the library. His silky hair shone. He was asleep now. Asleep and asleep forever. In the morning I took him to the vet's office. "Doesn't he look pretty?" I asked the woman at the desk.

"He looks beautiful," she said.

~

Now I HAVE ashes. And fourteen and a half years of our life together. And his leash and collar hanging by the door. And my heart full of the most beautiful, sensitive, intelligent, kind, sweet, adventuresome, athletic (except for the swimming thing), communicative, hospitable (except in relation to Lion) dog that has ever existed in the entire history of dogs. I told him all that on our last night together.

the wild cats

ONE DAY OF no wind, I looked out my back window to see tulips moving in the small garden next to the garage. I could see nothing moving them, and yet they continued to bend one way and the other, over and over. When I went outside to investigate, four tiny kittens ran into a hole under the garage. The hole looked like a small entrance to a cave. As I stared at it, a tiny yellow tabby returned to the cave entrance and hissed. All four inches of him. With great fierceness, he hissed again, then disappeared inside the cave.

AFTER I LEFT the garden, the tulips moved again.

I HAD SEEN a calico cat sitting on the walkway at the back of my garden for several months. "Feed her, and you'll have a cat forever," a friend suggested. But I had no intention of feeding her. The back yard was Blue's. For him and any visiting dogs. Although I regarded my friend Georgette's cat, Baron, as my friend, and, although I was used to her four cats, as a race, cats were foreign to me. One of their problems was that they were not dogs.

It apparently made no difference whether I fed the calico or not. She had moved into the space beneath my garage, an erstwhile nineteenth-century barn behind my small Victorian house. The space beneath the garage seemed home to several critters. Before the cats arrived, skunks had made use of it for several years. Even with the cats there, skunks still seemed to use it. Skunks are not fond of dogs, nor, after a first encounter, are dogs fond of skunks. But cats and skunks do all right together.

Once I saw the kittens, I decided that, cat or not, the calico needed to be fed while she was caring for the kittens. On the other hand, I also felt that with four kittens plus Mama Cat in the backyard, I would soon have four hundred kittens. Some weeks later, I called Connie, Bozeman's animal control officer, who often came to my house to pick up stray dogs who followed Blue and me home from the park. She brought me a live trap so that we could capture the kittens to take to Bozeman's no-kill animal shelter. They would be fostered out to become acclimated to humans, then adopted.

I set up the trap in the garden next to the cave. Two of the kittens entered it together, one black, the other dove-gray. Connie picked them up, brought a second trap, which we placed in the same spot, and took the kittens to the shelter. Almost at once, Mama Cat entered the trap. I think she was looking for her kittens. I took her to my vet to get her spayed and inoculated.

Two days later, Connie appeared at my door. The kittens, inoculated against distemper upon entering the shelter, had died of some new strain of distemper. The people at the shelter were upset, Connie was distraught, and I could not believe I had captured the kittens in order to send them to death.

"The others aren't going," I said.

"No," she agreed.

I picked Mama Cat up at the vet's and continued feeding her and the kittens. Sometimes I remained in the garden after setting the food out, to talk to the kittens when they came to eat. Mama Cat watched me from the cave entrance, coming to the food only after I had left. I stroked the darker of the two kittens with one finger while she was eating. At first, she left off eating and retreated to the cave. Eventually, she allowed the stroke. I never did more than that. A single touch.

One sunny afternoon, I was sitting on the wood plank floor of the deck behind the kitchen. Leaning against the brick, the bricks warmed by the sun, me warmed by the sun, I read. Something brushed against my back. Startled, I moved quickly away, only to find the dark kitten standing next to me, watching my reaction. She had come to offer friendship. I stroked her back with my whole hand. She rubbed up against me again. I stroked her. She lay down next to me.

How extraordinary—this invitation to friendship, this fearless acceptance of me in her life. I felt recognized. This little dark kitten saw me as trustworthy. No one could pay me more honor.

After that, she came running to me whenever I entered the yard. I continued leaving food near the cave for Mama Cat but began feeding the kittens on the walkway closer to the house. The dark one,

Calicat, ate comfortably next to me. (I named her Calicat because, naïve as I was about cats, I though any multicolored cat was a calico.) The tabby, Lion, was more cautious. Although he and Calicat did everything together, he waited at a little distance before coming to eat, to make sure nothing terrible happened to Calicat. When all seemed relatively safe, he rushed in to eat from the far side of the bowl, eyeing me all the while. I made no move to touch him.

Late in the summer, the skunks became more active. Hearing them outside my bedroom window at night, I decided they must now be living beneath the deck: summer quarters. I no longer let Blue out into the backyard at night. After I watched a skunk walk up the steps from the yard to the deck, I called Connie for another live trap. "For skunks," I said. I set up the trap on the walkway below my bedroom window, a few feet from the steps. At three in the morning, I heard the trap snap shut. "Got it," I thought.

In the morning, discovering I had captured Lion, I took him to the vet for shots and neutering. When I brought him back, I opened the carrier on the walkway in the back, near the cave garden. He walked out without looking back at me.

I knew I would have to take Calicat, too, but I could not bring myself to capture her, put her in a carrier, and take her. It seemed too large a betrayal of her trust. It was weeks before I gathered up the willingness to do it. When I did, it felt as much a betrayal as I had imagined.

~

At the vet's they asked me her name. "Calicat," I said.

"She's not a calico," the assistant said. "She's a tortoiseshell."

When I picked her up the next day and was handed the bill, her name was listed as "Tortikitten." Sort of a show name, I thought, continuing to call her Calicat. I figured she defined things differently than veterinary assistants.

~ე

IN THE TIME she was away, Lion, who had been away from her side only when he went to the vet's, was lonely. He came close to me when I brought his food. I petted him. He rubbed against me. He ate without watching me, then sat down next to me, the way he usually sat next to Calicat. I petted him longer. He climbed into my lap.

Lion was in the garden when Calicat returned the following day. Again, I opened the carrier at the bottom of the walkway. Lion came to her and the two of them sat down on the walkway. He lifted the front leg next to her and placed it around her, with the tenderness of a friend putting an arm around a friend.

I bought a bed for them and nestled it into the back of the doghouse Blue never used. I began feeding them next to the doghouse on the deck. When I saw a skunk eating from their bowl, I moved their food inside, to my bedroom, and left the door to the deck open for them. (Why no skunk ever walked in is beyond me. That one might have never occurred to me until I wrote this.) The kittens got used to being inside, and, at times, when Blue had gone out for a walk with a friend, they roamed about the house.

My mother, who had insisted on sharing her morning bagel with Blue ever since she and my father moved to Montana to live with me, now also gave pieces of it to Calicat and Lion. Both of them were leery even of her, who knew and loved cats, but they were interested in her bagel.

"You'll have to increase my bagel allotment," my mother said.

They played with the toys I bought them and chased one another around the house. Even Mama Cat became bolder. She came into the house to eat. She sat in the sun on the window seat. She sat next to me on the bed, content until I tried to touch her, at which point she was up and gone. She liked finishing the yogurt in my lunch bowl, and would linger next to me (as long as I did not attempt to touch her) on the deck where I ate lunch until I offered her the bowl. She tore a hole in the screen door, attempting to get into the house on a day when the bedroom door was closed.

～

AFTER MY MOTHER died, I told Mama Cat she had to stay healthy because she was the only Mama among us.

～

A YEAR LATER, I went to New York City for a few days. When I returned, Lion and Calicat greeted me, but Mama Cat was nowhere around. I was not really worried, because she had disappeared in the past, sometimes for several weeks, but had always returned. She obviously had some other sort of life somewhere. Her business. Calicat, on the other hand, rarely left the yard, never going beyond the alley behind the house. Lion left the yard only to cross the terribly dangerous main street in front of my house. (When they were kittens, Mama Cat had carried all of them across the street to my neighbor's woodpile. When I told my neighbor that four kittens had been born under my garage in May, she told me that four kittens had been born in her woodpile in May. They were, of course, the same kittens—born twice.)

A day after my return, Calicat came into the bedroom to eat and to visit. It was the last time I saw her. I checked with Connie and visited the animal shelter. I looked everywhere in the neighborhood. Something had happened to her. She would not leave me. No one else could touch her, let alone catch her. She would not allow herself to be captured.

The last time I had taken Lion to the vet for shots, the vet had pointed out beebees permanently lodged in the skin under his belly. So I already knew that some person in the neighborhood thought cats made good target practice. I could only assume that, perched on the fence behind my house, or across the alley, she had become someone's target. Nothing else made sense. Even if someone had captured her, she would not have stayed with them.

I missed her terribly. So did Lion. Did he know what had happened? It must have made no more sense to him than to me. He and I became closer. I continued to look for her. Even now, five years later and a thousand miles away, I continue to look for her, as if she will come walking down the driveway. Something in me cannot accept her absence, or the idea that she felt fear or pain.

When I moved to New Mexico with David, there was no question but that Lion was coming with me. I understood he was an outdoor cat, a wild cat, climbing trees and roofs, sleeping in his cave or the doghouse as he pleased, hunting birds, chasing insects. Eating inside, lying around on my bed, settling onto the expensive piece of cat furniture I bought him so he would have an indoor refuge high enough to be out of Blue's range did not make him an indoor cat. His whole persona was that of a free, wild animal. Life was his choice, not mine. He chose to be my friend, but friendship is not a domesticating process. It's just a way of working out a life, one of the infinite possible choices.

~

THAT INDOOR CATS live longer, healthier lives did not seem an adequate trade-off to me for robbing an animal of its freedom.

~

I CONVINCED MYSELF we could build walls around our New Mexico house too high for a cat to climb over. Yet I knew that Lion spent great amounts of his time walking around on my roof, or the roof of the barn/garage. Both were far higher than any wall that could be built. Then I decided that, after he had been inside for a couple of months, so that he knew where he lived, he would be able to return to being a wild cat.

It wasn't until we moved in that I discovered that the local coyotes ate any cat they can find. Lion would become an indoor cat. In exchange for wildness, he gets love. I wonder if it is anywhere near a fair exchange.

The day before we were to leave, I kept him inside and gave him Rescue Remedy. The good-sized dog carrier I had gotten for Blue when he was a puppy was large enough to provide sleeping space for Lion at the front and room for a litter box at the back. When I lowered the back seats of my vehicle, there was room for the carrier, Lion's furniture, his bed, food for the trip. He traveled five days like that. Every day I spent time in the back of the vehicle with him, taking him out of the carrier so he could move around freely. By the time we got to New Mexico, being inside a house must have seemed immense to him, compared to being inside the car.

I think he is not unhappy in New Mexico. I think that, in the same way Mama Cat had enough instinct toward houses so that she tore the screen door to come in, Lion has a sense that a house is not an inappropriate place to live. But I wonder if he thinks of Calicat, sister, dearest friend. I wonder if cats remember, or if life is so completely in the present that only the present exists. But then, why does he wait for me to come home when I am away? And why does he miss me when I am gone?

bosque del apache

❧

THE BALD EAGLE sat in the winter cottonwood. He turned his head toward me, then to each side, eyes ranging over the vast field of an eagle's vision, now staring into my scope, then back again and over again, so that he knew whatever happened in his world.

The bird count board at the visitor center said there were ten eagles in the Bosque today. It was late January, weeks before the current numbers of 25,475 light geese (mixed snow geese and the similar but smaller Ross's geese) and 10,520 sandhill cranes begin their preparations for the flight north. Not quite the height of their residency—that usually happens in mid-December—but still as many birds as my mind can hold. In mid- to late February, when cranes and snow geese begin their flights north, the eagles, too, head north. Or, as a woman who works at the Bosque said, "The eagles leave when dinner leaves."

I have seen many more eagles than ten in one place. One November, at the eagle gathering in Haines, Alaska, I watched 1,303 at the place where the glacier-driven Chilkat, Klehini, and Tsirku rivers come together in an upwelling of warm water. This water stays open all winter, allowing for the late run of chum salmon that attracts the largest gathering of American bald eagles in the world. When other food sources are frozen into the northern winter, the Valley of the Eagles offers sustenance and respite. Eagles have gathered here more or less forever.

But here, in the Bosque, where frozen glacial streams are not a problem, it is their small numbers that interest me, ten in relation to ten thousand cranes and twenty-five thousand light geese. By their scarcity alone they seem, to me, remarkable. (There are times when there are more. Ninety were counted several years ago, when an outbreak of avian botulism in the Bosque made for some easy eating. Eagles do not ingest the disease along with the birds. They do, however, clean up the mess.)

The Bosque del Apache lies along nine miles of the Rio Grande in the desert of south-central New Mexico, a 57,191-acre wildlife refuge, part of the U.S. Fish & Wildlife system, that safeguards habitat along the flyways the migratory birds use in their twice-yearly long-distance flights between the southern U.S. and Mexico and the northern U.S., Canada, and Alaska. The snow geese come from the Banks Highlands in Northern Canada, the greater sandhills from Greys Lake, Idaho, and some of the lesser sandhills from Siberia.

With the river's natural flood cycle disrupted, and critical wetlands lost by dams and draining, by settlement and invasive exotic growth, management of the Bosque involves imitating the river's once-natural flood cycles. Over fifty miles of ditches and canals have reclaimed extensive areas of this once-rich floodplain in the Chihuahuan desert. Impoundments mimic natural ponds. About 9,000 acres are heavily managed. From seventeen sandhill cranes wintering here in 1941 to 15,000 today, there is literal, living proof we can indeed *build* habitat that works. We can restore the intricate balance between wildlife and habitat, even if we cannot restore the wild landscape that once, on its own, offered all that was necessary.

The Flight Deck, a boardwalk extending out onto the edge of Impoundment 18-D, was constructed to accommodate the thousands of annual visitors who come to the Bosque to watch the tens of thousands of birds. It is where everyone gathers at sunset to watch light-geese and sandhills fly in from the cornfields to their night roosts on the water. The fly-in is a spectacular sight. Great streams of white geese fill the sky like ripples of glittering light, their excited calls as constant as waterfalls. The nights we watch the fly-in, snow geese and Ross's geese come in first, as if they want to settle on the water while there is still full light. At dusk, the sandhill cranes come, in pairs and groups and, as evening deepens, in increasingly larger flocks, wings moving in unison, the primitive, penetrating melancholy of their cries a counterpoint to the high, constant sound of the geese.

The order of fly-in is not sacrosanct. Sometimes the cranes come in first.

We chose the time of the January full moon for this visit, and now, sandhill cranes fly across the moon, descend to skim low over the water, their bellies glowing in the lowering sun, their wings dark above the sun, the flying birds reflected in the still pond, the long-legged silhouettes of cranes settled on the water reflected in the still pond. A primeval bird, made more primeval in the late light, rose light on the water, rose light on the butte beyond, the light of the beginning of time. The night seems settled now.

Then, suddenly, the sky erupts with birds. Snow geese rise from the pond to circle in every direction. Uncountable numbers of cranes arrive from the corn fields in the last moment of light. The entire sky becomes a vast, rose fluttering of wings and sounds. The cranes aim for the west end of the pond, huge primeval wings floating on the dusk; the geese sink like snowdrops on the east. Something rouses the geese again, and, again, they rise in the thousands, circling, circling over us so that we stand under a dense canopy of snow geese, until, circling, circling, they land on the pond in front of me. And then it is full night. The sounds recede into orphic dream, some ancient deliquescent wave of memory.

~

AT SIX THIRTY, the cranes stand in red pools of sunrise, immobile against the dawn. One walks across the shallow water. (The depths of the Bosque impoundments vary, but are usually between twelve and eighteen inches deep.) Another walks across the water. Then another. Each mirrored in the still pond by its shadow. The beginning of restlessness, of day. Ducks swim in the foreground, already feeding. A steady trumpeting of the cranes sweeps across the pond. Red sky eases into rose. The pond takes on its twilight colors of pale aqua and rose gold; the trumpeting increases.

Sun glows gold over the Oscura Mountains. Cranes stand in shadow. They stand in a pool of gold. At the edge of gold, a bald eagle roosts on a tall snag. The sun rises, blinding-gold on cloud layers rest-ing on the mountains. A second eagle roosts on a snag a few hundred yards away.

In the still early, cold morning, the geese begin stirring, their chat-tering growing more excited, more restless. A few take off, the signal for beginning. Then more and more lift off until, in a rush of wings and cries, hundreds mount the sky to fly in vast, undulating forma-tion, to the cornfields.

In mid-morning, I drive the Marsh Loop, a road of about seven miles that circles the main public part of the Bosque. Seeing what looks like an eagle's nest in a tree near a pond, I stop to check it more closely through my binoculars. A coyote walks into my vision, walks along the edge of the pond. A single coyote, then another and another, walking one behind the other along the pond's edge. The cranes standing in the pond move slightly further from the edge, further toward the pond's center, then resume their morning, as if the coy-otes were merely a breeze wafting by. The three coyotes I watch con-tinue into a stand of tall grass extending back from the pond. The third enters the grass, comes out to check the pond, enters the grass, comes out, enters, comes out, enters, and disappears.

The nest I take to be an eagle's is that of a great blue heron, a year-round Bosque resident.

Farther along the loop, I stop to hike a trail that leads through the Bosque, walking through winter woods to the river, the Rio Grande, the river we walk along in our own Corrales Bosque, the river of life in this desert. David and I walked here once with Blue, not long after we moved to New Mexico. All places I have walked with Blue hold his memory. It is not odd, then, that although I tell myself I am merely going for a walk, I am aware of looking for the three coyotes, as if they had been magic dogs.

⁓

THIS INCREDIBLE BIRDLIFE, and I am looking for magic dogs.

⁓

WEEKS LATER, IN March, David and I stand outside our house, watching a huge circling of cranes high up in the sky. Following the river north, they are on their way to a stop at the Alamosa Refuge in Colorado, then farther north to home. We had been watching groups of cranes in our own Bosque all winter. Fed by the Corrales cornfields, they roosted on the river in the early morning and the late day. Now they joined the thousands of cranes coming from farther south.

In 2001, we watched a snow-white sky over Denali National Park, Alaska, filled with cranes. It was late August. Thousands of cranes had begun their flight south from the Kuskokwim Delta. I have often heard the sound of a few cranes in Yellowstone's Pelican Valley and seen a few in flight. But thousands at once were new to me. I think they will always be new to me because there is no way your heart can prepare itself for the sight of thousands in the air. Since the beginning of autumn in Denali, and spring in the Bosque, I mark the year by the flight of cranes.

ripley's believe it or not

❧

WE HAD GONE to the Smokies for the Appalachian spring, the sweet pink profusion of redbud and mountain laurel, the mist-veiled valleys and peaks and the depths of green, the plunging waterfalls and rushing streams, the Edenic sense of country held in these ancient mountains. Fecund, is the sense one gets. It is hard to imagine, in the early morning presence of spring, in the promise of life spring brings, how endangered this place is. Air pollution from regional coal-fired power plants, from industry, and from the motor vehicles jamming park roads reduces visibility to less than a quarter of what it once was. Ground-level ozone and acid deposition threaten the health of park visitors and staff, of the very soil, of vegetation and streams. Nonnative pests and diseases are killing trees—the Fraser firs, hemlocks, dogwoods, beech, and butternuts—in a national park that, theoretically, protects about half the remaining old-growth forest in the eastern United States. It is easy to overlook all this (except for the traffic) in the wild abundance of spring.

In the process of working on a book about America's national parks, we stayed at a hotel at the park edge of Gatlinburg, Tennessee. Most of our time was spent in the park, hiking, but one morning when David, who is a photographer, was off working, I remained in town, curious to have a look at this tourist mecca, which is about as honky-tonk as a park gateway can get. Part American family vacation, part redneck, part country, part kitsch, all Southern, Gatlinburg bulges at its crowded seams.

As I approached the main street from a major cross-street, I noticed a man walking his dog on a lead. I had not seen many people walking dogs in Gatlinburg. National parks are not good places for vacations with dogs, because they are not allowed on trails. So I was interested in a person walking a dog in town. Then I noticed the dog wore something around his middle. At first I thought the dog had been injured, but as we neared one another I noticed a cat lying comfortably on padding wrapped around the dog like a vest. Seated on the cat's back was a mouse. The four of them walked up the street like that. All of them looked as if this was the most natural way in the world to go for a morning walk.

In front of Ripley's Believe It or Not! Museum, a tourist couple approached the group. They asked permission to take a picture. The man, the dog, the cat, and the mouse all stopped while the tourist snapped a photo. The man, who was wearing a broad-brimmed hat, removed his hat, subtly holding it out with the hand holding the lead as he ran the fingers of the other hand through his hair. As if he had only taken off the hat to rub his head. I was afraid the tourist, occupied by talking to the man with his dog, cat, and mouse, would not realize he should put money in the hat.

The tourist talked a long time without reaching into his pocket. I watched all this, *willing* the tourist to put money in the hat. I was so concerned with the tourist's behavior that I never considered my own. It never occurred to me until later that I, witness to the whole event, could also have put money in the hat. It was not, after all, just payment for the taking of a photograph. It was for the patience of the training, the idea of the training. It was for food for the mouse, the cat, the dog, the man. It was for imagination. It was for the peaceable kingdom. It was for trust.

For the remaining few days of our stay, I looked in front of Ripley's Believe It Or Not and on the streets of Gatlinburg, for the man, the dog, the cat, the mouse, so that I could put money in the hat, to make up for what I had let go. It is a year later now. I am 2,000 miles away. I continue to look. You never know where someone may turn up.

a few mules

BUCK, SIS, AND Festus really only cared how heavy their loads were; whether the loads were placed properly and tied so they wouldn't roll around; whether they could cadge mouthfuls of grass as they walked along; whether they could get unloaded fast enough to roll in the grass as soon as they'd like. I loved Buck, Sis, and Festus. I admired Rosie, whose life was spent trying to avoid being caught, but who worked like no animal on earth if you did catch her. Carrying an odd-shaped load, she could gauge how wide she needed to swing around a tree or a boulder. I admired her, but I never really loved her. She never came up to me when I was on my horse to rest her head on my knee like Buck did. She never looked deeply into my eyes like Sis, or listened to every word I said like Festus, although I suspect she never missed a thing that was going on. Dick, the outfitter who owned these pack mules, said she had been mistreated when she was young. I'm fond of Roberta and Beuford, the mules the outfitter pulled along with Rosie. His other mules, Beula and Daisy Mae, were too ornery for me. Once, when we were trying to load the animals onto the trucks to drive down to Yellowstone for a pack trip, we couldn't find Daisy Mae, who had pulled loose from the rail where she was tied and run off. I asked Dick if he thought someone might have taken her. "Serves them right," he said.

But Buck, Sis, and Festus were my mules, and I loved them. Ace didn't always love them. If any got too close behind him on the trail, he was apt to aim a kick their way, although, even then, he was somewhat tolerant of Buck, my lead mule. Sometimes Buck would lay his head on Ace's back and the two of them just stood there like that. I've watched them talk about things, Ace and Buck. About what, I'm not sure.

Pulling a string of mules is a serious responsibility. On narrow trails along the edges of cliffs, I had to make sure they didn't fall off. I had to get them safely across rivers and streams, which meant slowing Ace so that he wasn't plunging forward while they were pulling back in their attempt to keep from sliding off slippery, submerged rocks, or stopping Ace altogether as the mules made their careful way across a stiff current. I had to get them up and down steep hills and around sharp curves without getting their ropes hung up on trees, or any one of them on the wrong side of a tree. I had to make sure they got across fallen logs in the trail. Riding with one hand holding the reins and the other holding the rope to Buck, I watched backward half the time. Buck's rope under Ace's tail made Ace buck.

I learned that no matter how much you love a mule, it still does what it wants, although what it wants is apt to be closer to what you'd like it to do if it feels loved. (No amount of loving, however, can make any mule do a thing it knows to be wrong. Some people call mules stubborn. They are not stubborn. They are smart.)

I cannot imagine not loving your mules. You become so intimate with them, saddling them day after day, pulling their tails outside the saddle's breeching so that they can flick flies away, tightening the cinches enough that the pack won't roll, making sure the breast collar is secure enough that it won't rub and cause sores. Mules watch you do all this. They consider every move you make and let you know if you are doing it wrong by crying out a sort of sharp "hee" or kicking or turning back to look at you with exasperation in their lovely eyes. They do have lovely eyes. And magnificent ears.

My mules were small, so I could reach up high enough to pack them. Buck is a buckskin. Sis was a sort of gray-brown with a dark zebra stripe across her shoulders and another running down her backbone. Festus is a deep, deep brown, like bittersweet chocolate. My mules didn't match, but they were easy to identify out in the pasture.

I've watched outfitters working for the Park Service wend their way up Pelican Valley pulling strings of matched mules. I've watched the perfectly matched Forest Service mules that participate in every Montana parade, dancing their synchronized way up Main Street in Bozeman, so flawlessly choreographed that Balanchine could not have done a better job. Strings of matched mules are beautiful to watch—like watching *Swan Lake* where the corps de ballet consists of dancers all the same height. I guess my mules were all the same height, too—just different colors, different ways of being in the world.

In her last season of work, Sis began to have problems. She, so sure-footed, sometimes stumbled. She often seemed listless. At first, the vet thought she might have been eating too much lupine—a member of the poisonous pea family, like locoweed. *All* of the horses (and mules) grab mouthfuls of lupine as they walk through Yellowstone's gorgeously lupine-full meadows, if their riders let them. Ingesting too much causes an accumulation of alkaloid in the horse's body, poisoning the animal. The outward form of this poisoning can include staggering and bumping into objects, which Sis was doing. This didn't check out, though, and the vet couldn't identify anything else. We tried giving her time off, then tried not working her at all. We replaced her with Cheyenne, a wild horse adopted when she was very young. Cheyenne was usually given to a guest to ride, but she was also used to being in a pack string. I didn't like packing her because she was so round, it was hard to keep a saddle from rolling on her. It had to be readjusted and tightened, constantly. Besides, when I looked back, I did not see the three sets of mule ears I love—tall, flopping with each step, constantly alert and the only part of the mule you can see above the packs.

Sis stayed in the pasture through the end of summer and into the fall. Then she died. She was buried in the pasture where she died, a bit off from the meadows the other horses and mules used. It didn't seem possible to me that she would just die.

Death is hard for me to comprehend. To be in life one moment, in death the next, makes no sense to me. I try to see it all as a continuum, the one coming out of the other, out of the other and on into infinity. I try to remember the impermanence of all things, the illusory nature of life, but when someone I love dies, that perspective seems to go by the wayside. Perhaps this is why I am given so many opportunities to deal with death. Somewhere along the way, I am sup-posed to get it. But mostly, what I feel is just tired of death. A beloved animal's death. A beloved friend's death. The death of thou-sands of people and animals and cultures in unnecessary wars. All death. Except my own. That one I can deal with.

Maybe it is this necessary lesson that leads me to spend so much time, energy, and love on animals. Maybe this lesson is what my life is for.

five wolves

❧

I DROVE SOUTH to Yellowstone one December early morning, almost a year after wolves had been restored to the park. It was a gray, warm, gentle morning. A bald eagle flew toward me, low over the Yellowstone River. He was simply hunting, but I took his presence as an omen. I always take the presence of eagles as an omen. In the park, a soft rain fell, like the rain in Paris. As the road climbed upward, gray-white cloud veils drifted among the dales, chiffon scarves of some giant Isadora Duncan. I pulled off the road in the Lamar Valley, at the trail to Crystal Bench, and parked in mud.

A year earlier, before the wolves arrived, I was among a group of journalists invited to accompany the biologists Mike Phillips, Yellowstone Wolf Restoration Project leader, and Wayne Brewster, deputy director of the Yellowstone Center for Resources, to the Crystal Bench pen site, one of three places in the Lamar Valley where pens had been erected to hold wolves in the time between capture in Canada and release in Yellowstone. Lamar was selected because it is habitat for an enormous amount of game—that is, wolf food—but also because it contains the only road in the park open all winter. All three pens are a reasonable walk from the road. "For the first year, we wanted to make all of our mistakes from a blacktop highway," Wayne Brewster said. (The wolves that arrived the second year had two sites in Lamar, plus one on Blacktail Butte, and one, accessible only by snowmobile, on Nez Perce Creek, in the Old Faithful area.)

The pens, enclosed by ten-foot-high chain-link fencing, were about an acre in size. They had two-foot interior overhangs to discourage climbing over, and four-foot aprons at the bottom to prevent digging under the enclosure. Inside, there was open space, forested cover, and a few kennels, so a wolf could get away from its penmates. The entire perimeter was lined with electric fence, mostly to make sure nothing like a grizzly bear climbed the fence to find itself confronting wolves, with no way out for anyone.

The wolves arrived in shipping crates via horse trailer at the park's north entrance at Gardiner, Montana, on January 12, 1995. They were welcomed by schoolchildren bearing flowers, by government officials, wolf people, reporters, and ordinary citizens cheering their appearance. It was a moment of triumph for all who had long worked to return the wolf to Yellowstone, for the ecosystem, perhaps for the wolf itself. Yellowstone was, and is, a natural place for wolves.

A month later, I returned to Crystal Bench with a small group of journalists. From a hilltop about 300 yards from the pen, we were allowed a few minutes' view of the wolves—the time it takes for meat to be unloaded and hauled in to them. The quickness was necessary to avoid agitating the animals—who would be aware of our presence—any more than necessary. While meat was being loaded onto the same mule-drawn sled that had brought the wolves from the trailhead to the pen a month earlier, I asked Mike Phillips what was for dinner. He pulled out the day's menu: "quartered elk, a piece of deer." Wondering how the mules, who hate wolves (and all dogs), had felt delivering a load of wolves, I asked one of the drivers about it. "No different than any other load," he said. The mule drivers are packers for the park's north district during the summer. It's their job to get necessary stuff into the park backcountry.

"What would you normally be doing in winter?" I asked him.

"Drinking," he said.

On the hilltop, I had just time enough to set up my spotting scope for a fast glimpse of wolves pacing along the back fence before we had to leave. One jumped at the fence, but basically, they looked like big dogs waiting for their dinner.

On March 21, the pen gate was opened. None of the wolves left. When they did not leave the next day or the next, it occurred to the biologists that wolves do not recognize doors, so they cut a four-by-ten-foot hole at the back of the pen, where the wolves had consistently paced. Seventeen and a quarter hours later, a motion-detecting device indicated that something had passed through the hole.

And I understood wildness in a new way. Wildness is the absence of doors. It is unrestricted access to the earth by the earth's creatures. The Gardiner entrance to Yellowstone—the demarcation between civilization and wildness—is an arch without a door. But the pen had a door. The wolves, penned, had not been domesticated, not tamed, not taught about doors.

Biologists had predicted the wolves would exit the pens and high-tail it for the backcountry. They had said we would never see them from the road; that few people would ever see them; that we would be lucky, indeed, if we sometimes heard them singing.

Seventeen thousand people saw them in the first nine months after release. All summer and fall, large groups of people gathered along the Lamar Valley road, binoculars and spotting scopes at hand. And wolves came. I went out there a few times between backcountry trips, hoping I would see a wolf, although, in fact, I hoped even more that I would not. I did not want to see a wolf from the road. I did not want to be sitting in my truck, waiting for a wolf to come by. I wanted them wild, shy, away from us. I wanted to see one, hear one, in the wolf's territory. I thought for sure I would see one in the backcountry. It seemed impossible to me that I could spend most of the summer there and *not* see one, or, at least, hear their singing. Sometimes at night I listened so hard I could hear the stars move. I rode over much of the park, but I was not in the Pelican Valley when the Crystal Bench pack made their way there, nor on the Mirror Plateau for their arrival. By the end of September, I seemed to have been the only person in the ecosystem who had not seen a wolf.

On this December morning, as I walked in soft rain and sparse snow up sagebrush meadows toward the Crystal Bench site, I saw two cow moose on a hill. They watched me until, certain I was heading in another direction, they ambled on into the cover of trees. A raven cried. A wolf howled. I heard wolf song to the right, beyond the moose, beyond the trees. Then there was answering song to the left, beyond the hills, beyond the fathoming of things. I heard them call and answer, and I went on walking up the trail. Just before the hill that hides the pen, I stopped to look back at the meadows I had crossed. A hundred yards back, five wolves crossed my trail: three slightly ahead, a space, two more. Not rushing . . . just going somewhere. They disappeared behind a rise. I turned in a particular moment, and I saw wolves. I saw wolves in a wild place. I was alone and I saw wolves.

the dogs of corrales

⌒⌘⌒

Yorkie

ONE SIGN AT the entrance to town says, "This is an animal-friendly village." Another says, "Coyotes live in Corrales."

On my first visit to Corrales, I noticed recent horse shit in front of the hitching rail at the post office. The signs and the horseshit seemed reasons enough to live in Corrales, a still heavily rural town north of Albuquerque. While looking for a house, David and I stayed with Corrales friends at the edge of the Bosque. We walked our dogs together on Bosque paths every morning. The Corrales Bosque runs about seven miles along the Rio Grande, part of the Bosque running along much of the river. Or rather, the Corrales Bosque runs along the irrigation ditch, the clear ditch, the forest of cottonwoods, New Mexico olive, silver buffalo berry, willows and grasses; and *then* the Rio Grande. Muddy, sluggish, the Rio Grande is a river of history, of legend. It used to run almost 1,900 miles from its headwaters in the San

Juan Mountains of Colorado to its end in the Gulf of Mexico, the second-longest river in North America. Nominally, it still does, although dammed and regulated since the early part of the twentieth century, in the current years of drought, it doesn't always make it to its end. (Diversion dams, to supply water for irrigation, were built centuries before, by the Spanish, who arrived in 1540, and by Indians before them.) Nevertheless, in the Corrales Bosque, there is always some thread of it. Often the thread is meager, but sometimes—broad and fast and brown—the Rio Grande flows with its own memory of undammed rivers.

The Bosque boasts the highest density of nesting Cooper's hawks in America, which means there are plenty of small birds and mammals for them to eat. Sometimes, especially on the few gray, misty days, coyotes emerge from thickets along the trail or from farm fields on the Bosque's west border. Usually, upon seeing people, they slink off into underbrush between the trail and the clear ditch. Once in a while, they invite an unsuspecting dog to play, a lure to death.

On the far side of the Rio Grande, the side that borders land belonging to the Sandia Pueblo, there are eagles and sandhill cranes, ducks and Canada geese. All winter, the cranes and the geese glean corn from Corrales farm fields during the day, then return to the river to roost at night. When I walk down to the river, I often see one or two eagles on the limbs of high, old cottonwoods, from which they have views of the entire Bosque.

The Bosque is an oasis of wildness in one more area of America built too quickly, randomly. The Rio Grande is an actual river in the desert, but it is also a metaphor. It runs through the city of Albuquerque, a city eager to build at any cost, even though the arid New Mexican desert should not be asked to support the growth. Water usurpers and environmentalists clashed for a number of years over the use of Rio Grande water, although a recent compromise may make things work. The settlement—reached after more than a year of negotiations (and after a five-year court fight) between the Sierra Club, National Audubon Society, New Mexico Audubon Society, Defenders of Wildlife, the Southwest Environmental Center, and Forest Guardians on one side, and the Bureau of Reclamation and the Army Corps of Engineers on the other—creates a mechanism for the city of Albuquerque to lease, buy, and store water, allowing it to set aside about twenty percent of its water-storage space (about 30,000 feet) in the Abiqui Reservoir for water to be released into the Rio Grande during dry times. As John Horning of Forest Guardians says, the agreement is an attempt "to insure the river has rights to its own water."

The idea is for the water to maintain a permanent pool for wildlife—primarily the Rio Grande silvery minnow, an endangered species found only in the 233.6 miles of river flowing between Cochiti Dam north of Albuquerque and Elephant Butte Dam to the south. Some years, the water may not be enough. The agreement does not solve all of the problems of the river, but it is a start. Certainly it can serve as a model for cooperation.

There are many in the area who think the silvery minnow is nothing in the face of the household needs of the people of Albuquerque. "People or minnows?" they say incredulously, implying that environmentalists are totally nuts to think that water for people should be given to minnows. Even if they do not deem minnows equal to people in the general scheme of things, they are also not considering the silvery minnow as an indicator that the resources people need to live (and that livestock, wildlife, and vegetables all need) are getting used up. Too much water is taken from the river to serve the needs of too many people. No links in the chain of life are unnecessary. If the minnow becomes extinct, what else will we have lost?

People continue to water lawns. Developers continue to build subdivisions. But the biggest user, taking about eighty-five percent of the river's water, is agriculture. While most people in New Mexico would agree that chiles are an essential crop, trying to grow beef in the desert—that is, growing grass to feed cattle—is not the best use of desert, water, or, for that matter, a life. The agreement's water-leasing program provides the Pueblos—with first claim on the water—and Middle Rio Grande Valley farmers with payment for allowing their irrigation water to stay in the reservoir. For some farmers, this could be a way out of a losing proposition. John Horning talks about the necessity for a "populist movement to live within our means. I believe," he says, "questions need to be asked of agricultural practices in the desert."

In a certain way, to buy a house in Corrales—or anywhere in New Mexico, for that matter—seemed unconscionable to me. In another way, since the house was already standing, and somebody would buy it, it seemed better that it be people who care about the environment than, perhaps, people who would put in a lawn and a pool. Everything is rationalization. We needed a place to live in New Mexico. The fact of the Bosque—this sanctuary of wildness—made me think the place should be Corrales. I was impressed that people rode horseback to the post office. And I liked walking Blue along the river.

Mornings, the paths through the Bosque are thronged with people walking their dogs or riding their horses.

Before we bought the house, while still living in the borrowed house
of friends, our morning walk took us past a house with half a dozen
Yorkshire terriers. Each time we passed, the Yorkies ran out from some
hidden place, barking as if life depended on letting everyone know
they were there. The barks of one of them, the boldest and biggest,
a male, propelled him away from the driveway onto the dirt road, the
bark so all-consuming that it seemed to carry him onto the road by
its sheer power, the bark preceding the dog. Once we had passed, their
work was done until someone else came by. Blue and our friends' dogs
were all much larger than the Yorkies, but—terriers that they were—
the Yorkies had no concept of that.

One clear afternoon, a time normally quiet in the Bosque, Blue and
I walked along the path to celebrate the coolness of the day. At that
hour there were few people, although two women walked on the far
side of the irrigation ditch. A shepherd-mutt followed them, always
a few feet behind. He never seemed to catch up. A man bicycled past,
going the opposite direction. The dog turned and followed the bicy-
cle. I wondered at the women not calling him back. After a while, the
dog returned, once again following the women. "Is that your dog?"
I asked them.

"No, we don't know who he belongs to."

When the women and I, on opposite sides of the ditch, turned
back about the same time, the dog crossed the waterless ditch to walk
ahead of Blue and me. He was not at all interested in Blue. At our exit
from the Bosque, he was ahead of us. He remained ahead of us up

the dirt road past the Yorkies' house. The bold Yorkie ran out of the driveway, barking at the bigger dog. The dog lowered his head, picked the Yorkie up in his mouth, and began shaking it.

"Drop it! Drop it!" I shouted, running as fast as I could to them.

The dog shook and shook and shook the Yorkie who flopped around on both sides of his mouth like a rag doll.

"Drop it! Drop it!" I kept running and the dog took off running away from me, the Yorkie still in his mouth. He ran into the fields behind the house we lived in. There, at last, he stopped. He looked at me. He dropped the Yorkie. I ran to the Yorkie and the bigger dog ran up the fields away from the Bosque.

The Yorkie did not move. It would never move. I took Blue into the house, then returned to the Yorkie. It was only minutes since he had been alive, powerfully filled with his own life.

My friends Susanne and Jake drove up to their house across from the field. Crying, I called to them. They came quickly, Jake tenderly picking up the little, broken Yorkie. Fierce, fearless Yorkie. Biggest Yorkie in the world. Susanne called the Yorkie's people. As we walked toward their house, a man appeared, carrying a white garbage bag. He held out the bag for the dog.

"No, no . . . ," Susanne pleaded, horrified, as I was, at the implication that the dog was garbage. "Don't put him in the bag in front of her . . . she found him, she saw the whole thing . . ."

But it was too late. The Yorkie was in the garbage bag and the man turned and went home.

I never saw the bigger dog again. No one was willing to know who its people were, although there were conjectures. The Yorkies' people were relative newcomers in the community. In the end, it was just a thing that had happened.

That's not how I saw it.

The Unknown Dog

LION WALKED OUT the door left open. We had been in New Mexico only a few months, during which time Lion had not forgotten his beginnings as a wild cat. Besides, an open door is always an invitation. That world Lion could see through windows but was forbidden from entering, awaited. We had gone out another door for our morning walk in the Bosque with Blue and it wasn't until our return, over an hour later, that I saw the open door. I knew at once Lion had gone.

Cats should be outdoors. They are made for the outdoors, for climbing trees and hunting birds, for scratching in the earth, for lying in the sun. But, in Corrales, outdoor cats are eaten by coyotes. It is why there are no stray cats in Corrales. I often hear coyotes singing at night. One afternoon, a coyote walked across the bottom of our orchard. Another day, I watched one trot up the far side of the irrigation ditch paralleling our place.

I called Lion. I looked in the apple trees. I looked in the pines. I looked under things and inside things. There was enough time while we were gone for him to be anywhere. But this was new territory for him, huge and foreign. How much does a cat know a thousand miles from home, when he has only been inside?

I walked up and down the orchard, checking the trees a second time. As I came up the fenceline bordering the ditch, a vaguely mastiff-looking large dog appeared out of trees and brush on the far side of the ditch. Although several dogs had come up to the fence to investigate when I walked in the back with Blue, this was a dog I had never seen. He came toward me, looking directly at me all the time. He barked once. "Do you know where Lion is?" I asked, fearful he had caught him. The dog moved further up the ditch, stopped, turned to check I was following, barked again. I walked on my side, he on his. He stopped in front of a large tree somewhat back from the ditch and looked up. I followed his look. Lion sat on a high limb. The dog looked at me.

"Thank you," I said. "Thank you."

He turned and walked back the way he had come. I have not seen him since.

Shadow

BLUE HAD ENTERED his long process of death, becoming weaker daily. Crippled by spinal problems caused by the intense athleticism of his life, it was as hard for him to lie down as it was to stand. Medication eased some of the pain but did nothing for the confusion that the pain and old age caused him. I stayed up much of the night to help him stand when he wanted to stand, to go outside when he wanted to go outside, to try to ease his lying down. Both of us were exhausted. Hating to leave him alone in the house, I began attending to only the most necessary things. I continued the yoga class David and I share.

Partly because the yoga studio was around the corner and is a place of great peace. Partly because it was a way to breathe. Partly because the lessons dealt with the impermanence of all things and I needed to remember that neither Blue nor I were permanent and that impermanence is the creator of beauty, of death, of life, and of love.

Sometimes, during class, the teacher's Siamese cat sat at the glass door separating the studio from the dining room of the house. Sometimes he watched. Sometimes he slept. But his presence always made me feel that life was in order. I looked for him first, before beginning my warm-ups. One day a young, black standard poodle stood at the door instead. It stood looking in to the studio.

"There's a dog," I said to my teacher.

"I gave him to Judy as a present," he said. "I never really connected to dogs before, but he follows me everywhere and we've become friends."

"Can he come in?"

The teacher opened the door. The dog entered the studio and came to me without being called. He stood without moving as I held his face and buried my head in the thick curls that covered his head, that covered the entire dog. He stood like that, presenting me the comfort of his being.

"What's his name," I asked.

"Shadow," my teacher said.

~⌒

BLUE DIED A few days later.

～

FOR CARL JUNG, the shadow represented the dark side, the personal unconscious, the hidden, the things one "refuses to acknowledge" that are forever thrust upon one. The dark side is the place it is necessary to go to become whole. Does our fear of the dark represent a fear of our shadow? Is it our fear of the dark that creates our fear of death? There is no darker side than death, no place more necessary to go. However we fight entering the dark side in our lifetimes, there is, in death, no escape from it. Yin and yang form the whole. Light and dark. It was time for Blue to go. It was time for me to understand that.

When I asked, at our following class, if Shadow could come into the room, the teacher said he was not allowed in the studio. When I saw Shadow again, half a year later, he was shy and stayed away from people. Perhaps he had always been shy. Perhaps he came as Shadow that once, when it was necessary. I saw him as a kind of angel, leading Blue away from pain. Now I think differently. It was me he came to guide.

the drugstore cat

❦

MY FATHER'S DRUGSTORE stood at the corner of Spring Street and Plymouth Avenue, in Rochester's Third Ward, the historic section of the city, the "ruffled-shirt ward," whose old houses were built for large families and lavish entertaining. A 1946 reminiscence of the Third Ward in the quarterly *Rochester History* mentions that the "big, high-ceilinged rooms were at their best when their crystal chandeliers reflected the gas jets on the evening dresses and white ties of guests." The Third Ward was home to Colonel Rochester, founder of the city. Generations of his descendants lived there, neighbors to the writer of the reminiscence. There is snobbery attached to having roots in the Third Ward.

The drugstore was catty-corner from the Rochester Institute of Technology—producer of many of America's best-known photographers. RIT was the new, highfalutin name. Everybody in the Third Ward knew it as Mechanics Institute, purchaser of many of the huge old houses. Some it used. Some it tore down for space to build according to its own needs. "What price progress!" the memoirist mourns. The horse chestnut trees lining the streets covered that old neighborhood in a cool, green quiet. "Trees were everywhere in the Ward," the writer reminisces. "Sun dappled through, making orange lights and purple shadows on the bricks." My brother and I walked beneath the old chestnut trees, always returning to the drugstore with our pockets full of the large, glossy brown seeds exposed when their prickly burrs hit the sidewalk. I have no idea what we did with them. (They are called horse chestnuts because they were once used to treat respiratory ailments in horses.)

By the time I was old enough to spend time in the drugstore, some of the old families still lived in the Third Ward, although most of the houses had been converted to apartments or became the offices of organizations like the Red Cross. For us, RIT, where my brother and I sometimes served as models for the photography students, was more present than the history of the Third Ward. We just knew these were old buildings.

The drugstore had a soda fountain. Behind the fountain's stools, there were small tables and ice-cream chairs. It was the place everyone in the neighborhood came for lunch. The fountain was the hangout for RIT faculty and students and for reporters and photographers from the newspaper, a couple of blocks in the opposite direction from RIT. The only person who, inexplicably, never came into the drugstore was David, a first-year photography student at RIT during my last year of high school. (If we had met then, we could have been married 40 years longer than we have been. But then, who would we have been?)

To reach the drugstore from our house, we had to drive across the Genesee River. Sometimes as we crossed, my father recited poems to me, so that, ever since then, I have believed that rivers cause poetry.

～

THE DRUGSTORE HAD a cat. Nemo.

～

ONCE, WHEN I was sitting at one of the tables eating half a tuna sandwich, the cat climbed up on the table and ate the other half. I knew nothing about cats. I just knew that Nemo was my father's cat. Nemo's job was to keep in check any possible mice in the basement. The building was as old as all the other buildings in the neighborhood, all of them offering plenty of opportunity for mice. I hated going into the basement, with its narrow, ancient stairway and musty smells and odd pools of light from bare bulbs in the ceiling. The office, where accounts were kept, was down there. Once a week, my mother came in to the store to deal with the accounts. She went downstairs so I went downstairs, but I got back upstairs as soon as possible.

Nemo's job was not full time. He often lay in the display window, a good place to catch some sun and keep track of the activity on the street. I remember seeing him half-curled in a corner, somewhere near the KOOL penguin. I loved the penguin. With one flipper, it moved a cigarette back and forth to its mouth. Every time it removed the cigarette from its mouth, it blew out a circle of smoke. Nothing ever interrupted this.

In those days, keeping a cat in an establishment selling food was not illegal. Those were simpler days, when there was also nothing wrong with smoking. Cigarettes cost twenty-five cents a pack. I was never interested in cigarettes, but I found penguins fascinating.

Years later, after my father died, I went through the things he had brought with him to Montana. Among them, a scrapbook of his army days. There were photographs of other officers and men in his unit, of camp life, of Indians from the time he took his troops to Oklahoma and Texas—a postcard picture of Geronimo among the others. There were letters and invitations to army weddings and performances, letters to him from me. I was too young to write, but I dictated letters to my mother. Most of them told him how good I was and how my brother was bad. My brother was a baby and couldn't defend himself. There were letters from his Masonic order, offering whatever help they could. There were poems he had clipped from magazines and papers, all of which had to do with serving the greater good, honoring what is right and just, while turning one's back on greed and injustice, about the loyalty and patience of women, about the loyalty and love between man and dog. There were more poems about the love between man and dog than anything else. There was a tiny photograph of a cat seated on a scale in sunlight so bright, you can hardly make out more than the form of cat. And there were two yellowed newspaper clippings, neither with a date. The first of them is a photograph of a seated tabby cat, eyes focused on the photographer, left paw raised. Against a black background, his whiskers and the white on his face and chest glow. Beneath the photograph are three sketches of a seated cat. The caption reads, "A big sleepy gray cat which wanders aimlessly around a neighborhood drug store is a favorite model for art students at

Mechanics Institute. Here are some sketches made by Miss Brockmyre as she sipped soft drink at the soda counter."

⟿

Miss Brockmyre sketched Nemo in three different poses, each a drawing of grace.

⟿

The second clipping, on the verge of crumbling, is more fragile than the first. And more final.

> With great sadness we have to report that Nemo the cat is dead. Nemo was a very special cat, beloved of many generations of Mechanics Institute students, many residents of the Third Ward. Nemo was a drugstore cat pure and simple, born, brought up, fed, housed and pampered within the glittering confines of a modern pharmacy. He never ventured outside. He either sat in the doorway or in a window display of perfumes and soaps and watched the world go by. A few days ago, Nemo, aged 12, paled and sickened. He refused his daily hamburger. The fire was gone out of his soft eyes. Even when someone said, "Mouse," he paid no attention. They gave him some medicine, but in the night he went to cat heaven. Nemo was a great cat. We doubt that any of the three kittens being trained to succeed him will ever have his special personality.

penguins

❧

THE FLAT PLAIN from the beach rises into ice and snow ridges and snow-covered mountains. Thousands of penguins are scattered across the flats or snow patches or spring-brown earth. They stand in groups, as if talking. They walk back and forth as if on important errands. Sometimes they fall down. (Walking across crusty, slick spring snow seems as hard for them as for us.) When they fall down, they just stay down, sliding on their bellies, using their flippers in a swimming motion. Although their walk is often a little comical—a slight waddle with their arms (flippers) held out to the sides, their noses in the air— penguins are magnificent when swimming. Traveling long distances underwater, they propel themselves forward with their flippers, steer with their webbed feet. Deep, fast dives net them dinner—fish, squid, crustaceans—which adults eat only in water. (Chicks are fed regurgitated food on land.) Graceful, arching, porpoising movements allow them to breathe air. These are birds designed as fish.

A white sky descends over the mountains. The ocean crashes white against the black sand beach. Penguins stand among the prone bodies of elephant seals littering the beach. The seals look dead, lying on the beach like so much blubber, until one lifts a bulbous head or waves a flipper. A seal several hundred feet from us raises itself up and bellows. Steam pours out of its mouth. A young seal propels itself clumsily a few feet. A big bull heaves himself along the beach. Fast. It seems an improbable speed.

We have been warned to stay away from the seals. We are told they are quick to fight. For all the heavy permanence of their corpse pose, we are told they can quickly roll right over you, crushing you with their tons of weight. Indeed, they sometimes destroy penguin nests as they barrel across their landscape.

It is November in St. Andrews Bay, South Georgia. We have spent two and a half days on the South Scotia Sea, passing through the Antarctic Convergence, that place between Cape Horn and South Georgia that demarcates the line between earth as we usually know it and earth as cold purity. It has been a hard crossing through the wildest seas on earth, seas that circumnavigate the globe with no land anywhere to mitigate the force of wind. Early on, I thought I would die. Later, I hoped so.

St. Andrews Bay is a noisy place. The gurgling, burping, coughing, barking spitting of the seals; the humming voices of penguins like creaky doors that never stop; the surf crashing against the black sand beach. A little back from the beach, acres and acres of downy brown king penguin chicks—looking larger than adults—stand and wait. They look like tall teddy bears. Requiring their parents' care for up to fourteen months, these are last year's chicks, calling frantically for someone to come and feed them. Parents recognize the voices of their chicks, and vice versa, but because both parents go out to sea to hunt at the same time (unlike the parents of other penguin chicks), a chick can be left alone for weeks at a time. Kings range far offshore to find food. In winter, just getting offshore, when "shore" becomes a vast ice shelf, is a long process. Until their parents return, the chicks do not eat. If it takes too long, a starving chick may die. Or, if they do not return at all, their chicks will die. Nobody adopts orphaned penguins. We see several whose parents have not returned for too long. They stand, lean and hangdog, waiting on their feet to die. An occasional dead chick lies on the ground, ignored. The lucky ones, so fat they can hardly move, waddle tipsily across ground covered by rock and molted feathers. A glacier-water stream serpentines around the masses of penguins, an almost pastoral scene.

St. Andrews Bay was our second stop of the day. First thing after breakfast, we arrived at Grytviken, an erstwhile whaling port—empty, rusting, broken-down—a little to the north of St. Andrews Bay. In a gray day of gentle air, the sea was calm. We climbed out of Zodiacs near the whalers' cemetery and toasted Sir Ernest Shackleton at his grave. Any trip to Antarctica is a kind of homage to Sir Ernest, but when there is a Brit in charge, a toast is de rigueur.

Walking up a tussocky grass slope, we stepped around sleeping fur seals that looked like dark boulders. An occasional movement of a flipper served as paean to the difference between rock and animal.

Shackleton is not alone here. There are the men from the *Esther*, who died of typhus in 1846; the British magistrate who died after an avalanche pushed him into the icy sea. A large monument, standing slightly apart from the others, and facing due south in tribute to Shackleton's wish to reach the South Pole, marks his grave. At his wife's request, he is buried in this region of his dream.

All 104 ship passengers, plus the naturalists and some of the crew, stand around the grave, glasses of Bushmills whiskey raised in toast, as Peter Harrison, a world authority on sea birds, co-owner of the company conducting our tour, and a Brit, speaks.

"We Brits are a bit eccentric," he says. "We celebrate every disaster. Shackleton was a true Brit: he failed at everything. He always tried the impossible."

So far I have failed at seagoing. But I have always failed at seagoing. I used to get seasick on the Staten Island Ferry. I would never even have boarded another ship if it was not going to Antarctica, a place I have so longed to go my entire life that I forgot I get seasick. I note that everything at which Sir Ernest failed was heroic. I am not heroic. I am just grateful to be on solid ground.

I have begun wondering if there might be a way to stay on solid ground. Stay in Antarctica, live the rest of my life as a penguin. The longer we remain in Antarctica, the less far-fetched this seems to me. Most of the time when we land, I can't tell whether the figures walking in the distance are my shipmates or penguins. They all walk alike: arms a little out from their bodies for balance on the often-slick snow slopes, a slight waddle from the overboots we wear over footwear and under rainpants to keep us dry on the wet landings. But even up close, as the penguins stand in groups having what seem serious discussions—political, philosophical, meetings in the piazza—they seem quite like many people I know. I know we share more chromosomes with gorillas, but I'm certain our urbanity and civic consciousness comes from penguins.

(This is not implausible. Breeding colonies comprising tens of thousands of penguins make reasonable social interaction a necessity.) Quickly developing favorites among the penguins, I thought I might live among the Adélie. At just over three feet tall, the king penguin comes closer to my own size, but I find the smaller Adélie the most beautiful. (The emperor penguin, several inches taller than the king, comes closer still to human size. There are fossil records of a penguin that stood just under five and a half feet tall. But size is not the point here. Beauty is.)

The Adélie, named for the wife of nineteenth-century polar explorer, Jules Sébastien César Dumont d'Urville (I am not the first person to connect with the beauty of a penguin . . .), has a lovely white ring around its eyes that makes the eye look blue in a head entirely black. The black drapes down the Adélie's back and tail, and over its flippers. It is an elegant bird. As soon as an Adélie lays an egg, she takes off for two weeks at sea, leaving the male to incubate. This strikes me as a good deal. (The emperor penguin does this, too, only the male emperor, having not eaten during the two months of courtship, goes without eating another two months in order to incubate the egg during temperatures of minus forty, while the female travels out to sea to feed.)

The gentoo penguins also have a certain appeal to me. A little larger than Adélies, they have a white patch across the top of their heads, extending to the edge of their eyes. They are not as elegant as the Adélies, but they have a certain dignified charm. I like their name. And manners. The gentoo bows to its mate and sometimes brings a stone as a gift. Among penguins, stones are highly valued. They serve as currency, as nest-building material and, obviously, as love tokens. David frequently brings me stones, which, I think, serve all the same purposes. The gentoo is more of a homebody than most penguins, remaining near its breeding colony year-round. I, too, like being at home.

The chinstrap penguin, with its black "strap" under its chin, is comical, sort of like a London bobby, while the macaroni penguin, with pink feet and golden streamers on top of its head, looks peculiar to me. Sort of electrified punk.

It is the macaronis who provide us a view of penguin aggression. Visiting a macaroni colony at Hercules Bay the next afternoon, we step out of the Zodiac directly onto a rock cliff. Below us, the slick, dark rocks at water line are strewn with fur seals. We climb a steep snow slope to reach the penguins. On one side of the slope, seals lounge behind every grassy tussock; on the other, penguins busy themselves with the nesting process. A single penguin slips and slides downslope. Partway down he seems to think better of it (making me wonder about our own descent), because he turns to head uphill, waving his "arms" and moving up in little jumps.

On top of the slope, pairs prepare to nest while solitary penguins wait for their mates to return. *If* their mates return. Among the rocks and grass tussocks are thousands of penguins, their cries sounding like a motor being primed. A young male lifts his head in ecstatic display. "I'm here," he calls. "This is mine! This is mine! Who wants me?" Suddenly, voices erupt into angry volume as two fight. Pecking and pushing his adversary, the dominant penguin fights without mercy. The two slide downhill past me, the winner on top of the bloodied loser, the victor never letting go his hold on the loser's beak. Later, after the two climb back up the slope, the winner walks quietly up to the loser and, once again, attacks him.

We began this day with a hike up part of Shackleton's route across South Georgia, after his ship, the *Endurance*, became ice-locked in the Weddell Sea. The *Endurance* had left England for Antarctica on August 8, 1914. On January 18, 1915, it became ice-locked. Drifting with the pack ice for ten months, it was sunk by crushing ice in November 1915. In December, Shackleton and his 27 men began pulling the ship's three lifeboats across ice for almost 200 miles before reaching open water, then headed for Elephant Island, arrived on April 15, 1916, and set up camp. Nine days later, Shackleton and five other men left for South Georgia in the *James Caird*, a twenty-two-foot lifeboat. Eight hundred miles in the open sea. In the Antarctic winter. Making landfall on May 10, he and two of the men then crossed the island's 6,000-foot mountain range to reach Stromness, a whaling station—and help—on the opposite side of the island.

Our hike, from Fortuna Bay to Stromness Bay, is four miles long and in Antarctic spring. Theirs—from King Haakon Bay to Stromness—took thirty-six hours. Ours takes part of a morning. We climb 1,100 feet in a heavy snowfall, trudging uphill into a world entirely white—sky and the earth the same white. The descent is far steeper than the climb, although by then, in full sun, the day has become hot. We tie our jackets around our waists, sit down and slide much of the way to the bottom on a route slick as ice after the first walkers in the group have tamped it smooth. Instead of whalers at the end of our route, we find a colony of gentoo penguins. Some are building nests of mud and grass. Some are sitting on eggs.

On Prion Island, we run a gauntlet of seals on a narrow corridor the naturalists set up so that we can get beyond the beach. Using long poles, they urge the seals to the sides of the impromptu path. The seals snarl at one another and glare at us with fight in their eyes as we pass.

We come upon an array of albatross nests on the tussock-grass hillsides we explore. Many of the albatrosses we see are dark brown juveniles who, after 274 days on their nests, are about to take off for eight-year flights, before returning to their nests as black-winged white adults. They will stay at sea for eight years, eating what the ocean offers, sleeping afloat on its surface. The eleven-foot wingspan of these largest birds in the world are adapted for long flights over open ocean. I wonder at the albatross's initiation into life, what it knows, how it knows. Does it anticipate the next eight years? What timing keeps it flying all that time? What is its inherent need to wander? What does it feel on return, at last, to nest? I am fascinated by these birds— by their beauty and the wandering nature of their lives. The eight-year inauguration into what it means to be an albatross strikes me as a thing to emulate. The years of its life prepare it for its life. Everything is part of the whole. I think about my own education. Did it come anywhere near being so complete?

Several adults, returned from their time at sea and ready to nest, look at us without fear. One adult rises on its nest like an enormous angel, white head and body and spread wings—white on the undersides, with black outlining the trailing edge. It is huge against the brown tussock-grass.

Although in some ways, the albatrosses seem a side-trip (i.e., they are not penguins), in another, because they are spectacular birds possessed of a dignity born of amazing experience, because they are iconic, and because they are endangered, they become one of the most vital aspects of this trip. Walking among their nests, we engage in their beauty.

~

I AM SORRY to leave them. Especially since, both in returning to the ship and then disembarking a few hours later at Right Whale Bay, we are, again, surrounded by seals. Feisty fur seal males and females and pups and fornicating elephant seals. Scattered over the snow backing away to the mountains and up the snow slopes, seals lie like glacial erratics or slide along the snow like some primeval flowing sludge.

Huge gatherings of penguins are everywhere, too. Penguins move from one group to another. A solitary penguin walks down to the photographers to see what such creatures might be doing. When David kneels to take a photograph, he and a penguin stare at one another, eye to eye. I wonder what the penguin thinks. Does it interest him to see us? Does he think we're birds? Does he think the camera is part of David? (*I* think the camera is part of David.)

I love the penguins and hate the seals, who look brutal to me. Would I think they look brutal if we hadn't been warned what fighters they are? Can I be so easily swayed? Such prejudices are inappropriate. Seals are seals. Penguins are penguins. Perhaps I am not taking in enough. Did I not witness dignity and acceptance in the albatrosses? Was my visit to their nests *that* superficial? I am enthralled by this cold world—cold sea, cold wind, blue-cold ice floating past, gray sky, soaring dark cliffs revealed beneath white snow and blue ice, a pale sky ahead of us, a weak light on rock and ice, a weak light low in the gray cloud sky, snow-white birds, snow on the ship's railing, snow on the icebergs and the islands and the peninsula. Some of the largest icebergs through which we pass look to me like cities built of crystal, dreamscapes holding hidden glittering worlds. The huge sky belongs to the sea. The gray sea belongs to the sky. Albatross and penguins and seals are all a part of the whole. Nothing could be missing. I have no idea what to do about my bias.

~

A HUGE FIGURE of a dog, limned by stones and surrounded by snow, lies embossed on a hillside, a drawing of nature, etched by melting snow. A terrier. I wonder if it is a message about Blue, who is at home, struggling with old age. Some days later, an e-mail message arrives for a friend on the trip whose Corgi has died. The vet did what he could to save the dog, the message says. I don't think I could bear it, if there was a message about Blue. So much for staying forever and living as a penguin.

We arrive at Elephant Island after two days of cruising the South Scotia Sea through floating ice and icebergs. Shackleton's men spent 137 days on Elephant Island. I cannot imagine their waiting. And yet, they *knew* that Shackleton never failed to take care of his men. Maybe this is the only real success. To be first to do a thing is nothing. If one person doesn't make it, the next one will. Being first is just a game, a nationalistic moment of triumph. Caring for the people or animals who give their all in the face of failure is the deepest humanity, an antithesis of nationalism. If only all of us could fail as Shackleton did . . .

A light snow falls. Icebergs heave up and down in the sea, as if the sea were breathing. There are rounded bergs and spires and arches, blue ice on some, dark silt on others. All the cracks on Elephant Island's massive, uplifted, and tilted dark rock are defined by snow. Chinstrap penguins are everywhere—atop the rock ridge we face as we Zodiac in to the island, and on the snow slopes. Five penguins stand on a snow cliff overlooking the sea. A leopard seal swims below the cliff. The penguins lean forward, arching the tops of their bodies as they crane their necks to watch the water below. Suddenly, a piece of the snow cornice gives way and one penguin falls into the water. A second one falls in. The three remaining penguins look down toward the water, necks arched, feet firmly back from the edge. We land at Wild Point, campsite for Shackleton's men. Chinstrap penguins surround the monument erected on the island to celebrate the rescue of the men on August 30, 1916, by a Chilean navy cutter. (The monument was erected by the 24th Chilean Antarctic Scientific Expedition in 1987–88.) Chinstraps are everywhere, on snow, on rock; thousands of them walking back and forth, flapping their wings, raising their heads in call to mates.

As we return to the ship, the leopard seal swims next to the Zodiac, one of the penguins that fell when the cornice gave way in his mouth. The penguin is not dead. Not quite dead. The seal plays with it the way a cat plays with a bird, shaking it, tossing it up, grabbing it again, swimming along with the Zodiac, as if to make sure we all see. When he drops the penguin within the boatman's reach, the

boatman—instinctively—against regulations (and his naturalist training) that direct leaving wildlife alone—grabs it and throws it into the
Zodiac. A flopping, half-dead penguin. One flipper is broken. One
eye is gone. It will not live. Realizing he should not have interfered,
the boatman throws the penguin back. The seal reclaims his prize.

There is a natural order to life and death. We prefer not to witness
it. It is violent, irrevocable, messy. One among ten thousand penguins,
and yet, it seems so personal. Every death we witness is personal,
something that happens to *us*. A small black seal pup lying by himself on a beach, whose mother has not returned from fishing, is
dying. We can see death claiming him. Nothing covers up death in
Antarctica. Maybe that is part of the purity here—the clarity with
which we see death and life as part of the same process. Who lives,
lives among death.

Small groups of Adélie penguins float by on icebergs. A strip of
orange light lies on the horizon. A cold wind floats like the icebergs,
like the sea, like light. Three whales swim past. The ship moves slowly
through ice in a narrow passage, floating ice banging against the
prow and sides. We swing out around a huge berg in the middle of the
passageway, scattering flocks of birds settled on ice-free water, scattering the huge, cold silence of their world.

We do not enter this world on its terms, but from the safe comfort of this small ship. We look at this world as we look at captive animals in a zoo, a wonder, a curiosity. Maybe that, more than the
seasickness that will not leave me, is why I want to live as a penguin.
I am a good tourist when it comes to looking at architecture and art
and the narrow streets and walls of ancient cities, but I find it difficult

to look at animals or mountains as curiosities. (Having curiosity is an act of imagination. Seeing a thing *as* a curiosity, as if it were there for one's entertainment, seems to me a failure of compassion.) I find difficult the disconnect inherent in viewing nature as curiosity.

The photographers on board wish to capture all that we see. They will return home with marvelous images, but I am unable, as I always am, to understand how you capture a moment in the earth's history when the moment itself is transitory and the essence of this place is the ongoing wild silence of its history. In the instant of capture, it is already false. I have loved photography since I was a child. (The only Girl Scout badge I ever earned was in photography. My father set up a darkroom for my brother and me, and I was fascinated by watching images emerge from their baths.) I loved David's photographs for years before I met him. But I think I really do not understand photography. I do not understand the capture of time.

The ship swings out again to avoid five large, tabular icebergs. We head toward vertical rock cliffs. Directly ahead, pale sun on the snow and on rock mountains. So pale a sun. The ship turns into a narrow channel, passes through to clear water, where we come upon a blue berg with a large archway, like a gateway from one moment in sea-time to the next. A wind rises. Ripples spread across the mirror surface of the sea. A range of mountains appears, their façade veiled by stripes of gray cloud interspersed with pale blue sky, like the dawn of frozen earth.

In the Zodiac with the motor off, we are aware of the gentle lap of calm water. Off Enterprise Island, in a calm bay surrounded by snow slopes, we float into a garden of icebergs, upturned and carved—blue ice, deep, deep blue in the cracks, intense green-blue at the base.

What is miraculous here is the silence. On the ship, and, usually, in the Zodiacs, the sound of motors is omnipresent so that, until now, we have not heard the sea. The lapping of the water offers us eternity. The scent of water and ice is as cool and pure as the blue ice and unbroken snow. Sometimes the thundering sound of a calving glacier interrupts the clear silence, the gentle lapping. Seen. Unseen. The movements of earth that happen whether we are here or not.

The earth is so deeply present in Antarctica.

~

OFF THE WEST coast of the Antarctic Peninsula, we circle a huge, castellated berg, carved in lines and circles and plates, knobs and prows and cornices. We motor into an area of a bay rife with ice sculptures— small bergs carved into figures of animals and abstracts. Two gentoo penguins sit on a snow slope behind the sculptures. On the glacier wall at the edge of the bay—crevices of deep ink blue. The water is shallow and clear here, and we can see rocks and pebbles lying on the bottom.

We cruise a narrow channel, closed in by mountains and glaciers. Brilliant sunlight glitters on mirror-still water, on bergs and ice floes. We pass Danco Island, site of a Chilean research station in the 1950s. Gentoo penguins stand on the island's rounded snow top. Beyond this island, the land is Antarctic proper.

Reflected in the mirror sea, the jagged snow and glaciated mountains we approach are blinding white in this sun. A cloud-mist hanging above the mountains renders amorphous the line between cloud sky and cloud land, the one easing into the other, all of it like angels' wings.

Until now we have walked on Antarctic islands. This afternoon, we step onto the continent itself. For all my wish to come to Antarctica, I never imagined I would be so moved by stepping onto it. I climb out of the Zodiac and onto land and cry for the sheer, huge beauty of the land; the huge beauty of the *idea* of the land; the crystal, luminous, numinous, untouched purity of it; for arrival at a place I deeply wish to be. I cry for knowing I am here. In this place, I have seen the earth intact.

~⌒

GENTOO PENGUINS MEET the Zodiacs the way people in remote island harbors meet incoming ships: for the variety they offer the day. The penguins walk up and down the same paths we use (or, rather, we are using their paths), carrying stones in their mouths to build, or augment, nests, entering the water to cool themselves and to clean their feathers, which do not function properly when dirty. Many of the penguins are quite muddy, because the central part of the colony is a deep brown-red mud. The nests of the experienced penguins are substantial, like little stone buildings. Those nesting for the first time, relegated to the outer edges of the colony, have a ways to go. Two penguins argue over a nest. One must have attempted to take it over. That one was sent back to a much less impressive nest below the disputed one.

Penguins steal stones from one another. The treatment of a caught thief is harsh. After watching the macaronis at Hercules Bay, I would not be willing to risk getting caught. But then, the thought of getting caught has always deterred me from a life of crime. When the nests are ready, the penguins lift their heads in rapturous braying. They sound like mules.

David and I have climbed high up on the slope overlooking the bay, settled into soft snow in brilliant sun. We are watching the movement of penguins, the sun on the sea, the ship far below us, a skua on a rock ahead, about halfway up this slope. Skuas, large, gull-like birds with dull brown feathers, often nest near penguin colonies. Extremely territorial, they defend "their" penguin nests from other skuas. Suddenly, this skua flies into a nest, grabs an egg, flies downslope away from the penguins, and begins to eat. I wonder if everybody in Antarctica is a thief. Maybe that's how you make a living here. But I think skuas are cleverer thieves than penguins. I watched a pair operate in an Adélie colony. One wandered the edge of a nesting area while a second perched on a rock in another area, watching. The first one pecked at an old egg shell, distracting the penguins, who are always on guard against thieves—skuas; other penguins; snowy sheathbills who will trick them into dropping food, then steal it. What else? Quickly, the second skua moved to the back of the area, grabbed an egg, and flew off. His mate left the decoy egg shell and followed.

In yet another colony, we watch a skua fly to a hillock near us with an egg in his mouth. Laying it on the rocky ground, he pecks at it. His mate takes over. She moves the egg. The egg rolls. She picks it up quickly, moves it to another spot. It rolls again. She catches it, picks it up again and the two of them settle in for a meal.

Although I find skuas intriguing, I have developed a prejudice against them akin to my prejudice against seals, leopard seals, particularly—even though, in the ranking of crime, stealing an egg seems less dire than killing a penguin. I know that all of this is simply life. Skuas and seals need to eat and rear young as much as penguins do. Predators must be supported in their original habitats, for, without them, the unchecked growth of animals who do not eat meat will destroy any habitat. Life lives from life. Nature left to itself is a place of balance. Animals fill niches, but they are not colonialists. Any true naturalist would be as interested in the leopard seal as in the penguins. It has been easier for me to come to grips with the skua, perhaps because it is a prettier animal than a seal. I wonder how shallow I am. In any case, I am certainly partisan, a biased observer. Apparently it doesn't take much to sway me: just a tuxedo-clad bird I'd like to dance with.

At Anvers Island, we visit Palmer Station, one of three American research stations in Antarctica, this one devoted to studying long-term ecological events. Biologists here have marked half of nearby Torgerson Island off-limits to tourists and left them access to the other half, in order to study the impact of tourism on the island's Adélie colony. It has been divided for years, but, so far, they have found nothing to indicate tourism is bad for the penguins. (So, obviously, my permanent presence will not have an impact on the penguin colony.) We tour Palmer Station in the company of a young American from near Dayton, Ohio. I went to school near Dayton, Ohio. At the end of the tour we enter the kitchen, where we are served coffee and brownies, and another American tells us he worked at McMurdo Station and the South Pole Station before coming here. "Where are you from?" we ask.

"Arizona," he says, with obvious relief at having escaped the heat.

～

ON THANKSGIVING DAY, after nine days at sea, rebuffed from Paulet Island by serious ice, we head instead through uncharted waters to Gourdin Island. The ship's captain, delighted to be plying uncharted waters, parks the ship into a tabular iceberg. As we approach our landing, we notice a leopard seal patrolling just off shore. Large groups of Adélie penguins stand on every ice promontory, ready to dive in, but aware the seal is there. Craning their necks forward while standing back from the very edge, as if wary the edge could break off, catapulting them into the sea, they are watching, waiting. In the constant low murmur of their voices, they seem to be discussing the ramifications of diving in. Yet, many penguins are already in the water. The penguins on the promontories seem as interested in the penguins in the water as they are in the seal. The penguins in front suddenly decide to chance it and, arcing like a waterfall over its irrevocable edge, they dive. Those standing back from the edge now run forward—although not *too* forward—craning their necks to see a group porpoising by. The murmur continues. Meanwhile, the leopard seal catches a penguin, then swims to the inlet created by the bergs, the penguin in its mouth.

I am becoming better at this. The sacrifice of one penguin means freedom for the others. One of tens of thousands. The freedom is only for the moment, but everything is relative. To eternity, individual life is no more than a moment. A simple act of nature provides life for the seal and death for the penguin. Watching the next wave of penguins diving into the ocean, I begin to understand that death is not personal.

coyotes in yellowstone

❦

ON OUR WAY TO Cooke City, Montana, in late January, we stopped in Lamar Valley to watch coyotes hunting mice. Every time we saw a coyote trotting by itself across the vast snow meadows of Lamar, we pulled over and grabbed binoculars. (So eager to see wolves in Yellowstone have people become that they often translate coyote into wolf. Coyotes are smaller than wolves. Although from a distance it is not easy to gauge size, a good guide is that coyotes are usually alone and wolves are usually not. Also, in Lamar Valley, hordes of people line up for hours behind spotting scopes where there are views of wolves and nobody bothers with coyotes.)

On both sides of the road, we watched hunting coyotes stop in their tracks as, apparently, they heard the sounds a mouse makes scurrying beneath the snow. Through my binoculars, I could see the intensity of the animal's listening. Once an exact location was pinpointed, the coyote often took a few steps to get into a better position before springing into the air to pounce on the mouse with its front feet. Sometimes the coyote pounced several times, occasionally digging as well, before coming up with a mouse in its mouth. Although the hunting is serious business, the movement of springing and pouncing looks so playful that it always surprises me when I see the mouse.

In his 1940 monograph on the ecology of the coyote in Yellowstone, Adolph Murie reports watching a coyote capture and eat eleven field mice in an hour and a half. When conditions are right, and mice abundant, the coyote can survive on them even if the snow is over a foot deep.

Clearly, on this day, conditions were right.

ALL THE HUNTING coyotes we saw looked healthy and well fed, with thick and lustrous fur. The sad, scrawny animal we came upon on the road as we drove on from Lamar to Cooke City seemed to come from another world. Head down, he skulked down the middle of the plowed roadway like some cast-out, shrunken animal. His coat was thin and dull. His ribs were visible. His hunger was visible. There was no pride in him, no prowess for the hunt, no spirit. Walking the road was easier than negotiating the meadow snow, even though the meadows would have produced the sound of a mouse. We slowed down as we approached him, uncertain whether to try passing on one side or the other, or just meld our timing into his.

In his steady plodding down the road he seemed unconscious of us and yet, he could not have been unaware. Beggar, conditioned to human food, habitué of the Cooke City garbage dump or recipient of human handouts, nothing in him reminded him of his magnificence, of his role, in the naturalist Hope Ryden's words, as God's dog.

In 1990, a team of biologists began studying medium-sized mammals—coyotes among them—in Yellowstone's northern range. Their objective was to collect data on the region before wolves were reintroduced, so that it would be possible to gauge the difference the presence of wolves made on other animals. Wolves—along with coyotes, wolverines, lions, and other predators—had lived in the area of the park before being extirpated as "bad" animals after Congress passed legislation, in 1914, eliminating all predatory animals from public lands, including national parks, but no one had taken notes then. Coyotes had been included in Yellowstone's (misguided) attempt to rid the park of predators to make it safe for "good" animals—elk, deer, and antelope—but extirpation doesn't take on coyotes. Ever. Survivors under any circumstances, the coyotes come back no matter how much they are poisoned, shot, or trapped. In fact, coyotes come back stronger than before, which is probably why they are so major a figure in Indian tradition. The coyote's role for Indians is that of teacher and trickster, a kind of vital spirit that both initiates and pervades history. In Yellowstone, coyotes, who had long filled the wolf's vacant niche, were expected to feel the newly restored wolf presence the most.

The policy of extirpation continued in Yellowstone through the winter of 1934–35, although it was officially reversed in the national parks in 1933. Outside the parks, extirpation continued on public lands until Congress passed the Endangered Species Act in 1973.

Once wolves were eliminated, the Yellowstone coyotes, with a plethora of winter-kill to feed upon, as well as an inordinate number of rodents year-round, and no competitors anywhere near their equal, became bigger, sleeker, and braver than coyotes in most places.

For the five years of the pre-wolf study, biologists compiled simple inventories of animals, noting where they were and what they were doing, in order to compare what would happen in the presence of wolves. Mixtures of various odorous things were put on high branches, to lure animals into the area. Searching for the source of the smell, the animal would find one of the two dozen wire snares set up by researchers, enter to take the bait (an event that could take days or weeks while the animal decides whether the risk is worth the danger), then leave a few hairs caught on the wire. Because every animal's hair is different in color, structure, and texture, it is often possible to identify an animal by a single hair under a magnifying glass.

In addition to the snares, researchers used about a dozen cameras set up in major drainage points where streams enter the Yellowstone River. The cameras, developed for hunters to monitor big-game animals before the season, take a date-stamped picture when an animal goes for bait and breaks a red beam sent from a transmitter to a receiver.

Coyotes were trapped and radio-tagged. Adults were fitted with collars, while eight- to twelve-week-old pups had small, capsule-like transmitters implanted in their abdominal cavities by a wildlife veterinarian who set up his surgery tent near the den site. The surgery took about fifteen minutes, after which the pup was returned to its mother. For the animal, this method was far less invasive than wearing a collar and antenna the rest of its life.

It was less invasive for me as an observer, too. Any time I saw a collared coyote in the park, I thought it was somebody's dog—illegally off the leash, at that. Antennas sticking up from their collars made them look as if their people came from Mars. Of course, collars or not, coyotes (and wolves and foxes) *are* dogs, and biologists studying them—like the rest of us—relate to them as dogs. In an attempt to maintain some emotional detachment, the biologists designate individuals by numbers rather than names. I doubt this actually works. It did not work for Stefania and me at our peregrine hack site. Referring to them by the colors of their leg bands, in quest of emotional detachment, simply turned adjectives into proper names. *Any* word or number can become a name. Naming things engenders attachment.

I suspect emotional detachment when working with animals is not possible. Why would you elect to study a particular animal if you did not *love* that animal? You do not spend a lifetime studying coyotes or wolves or eagles in order to learn something about humans—although, of course, you learn a great deal about the particular human that is yourself in the studying. Maybe scientists working in labs with rats can free themselves of emotional attachment, but even rats have their own personalities. I once saw a rat soon after she had given birth to what looked like about fifty babies. (This *could* be a slight exaggeration.) She lay on her back in her cage, all four legs splayed out, head lolling to one side, eyes closed, in a posture of utter exhaustion. How *not* care about her?

The transmitters allowed researchers to track individual coyotes, each of whom had its own radio frequency. Observers learned which animals were dominant, which had pups, which dispersed, which were eating what, what coyote pairs were doing.

Studying an animal thoroughly is deeply satisfying. Satisfying to our curiosity? Adding to our knowledge of all life? Catering to some need to know how every living creature manages its life? Yet, isn't there also some need beyond scientific curiosity to never know *everything*, so that wildness retains at least remnants of its mystery, its own life?

On a cold morning in February 1992, I snowshoed in Lamar Valley with a Yellowstone Institute class studying coyotes. Brilliant sun magnified the depths of cold. Ice vapor hung on the clear air like a veil, ephemeral and translucent. It was the kind of cold that makes your nostrils stick together when you breathe. When we picked up a coyote track almost at once, I welcomed the warming effort of following it uphill.

The coyote walks in snow with the same intelligence he uses in everything else. To conserve energy, he places each of his feet in a straight line so that he steps in his own already-compacted footsteps rather than entering deep snow separately with each foot. The straight line breaks at any spot where, hearing a mouse beneath the snow, the coyote stops to pounce on it. In the absence of larger fare, rodents provide much of coyotes' food. In the presence of abundant food, it must be sort of like eating a really good cookie.

A distance from us, and higher up, in an open space between two edges of forest, we saw two coyotes and several elk. When the coyotes disappeared into the woods, we followed the track away from them, so as not to come too close and disturb them. As we crossed the expanse of snow meadow, we saw a coyote above us, trotting off with an elk leg in its mouth. We climbed up into the high forest to find the carcass.

The dead elk was a calf of the year. Our instructor cracked open a bone to reveal marrow that was red and gelatinous, a sign that the elk was in poor condition. In a healthy animal, the marrow is thick and pinkish-white. The elk had bite marks on its nose, indicating it might have been brought down by coyotes, rather than have died of starvation, although, clearly, it was on its way to that death.

How far away this poor, miserable animal walking down the road was from that vibrant animal I saw walking into the forest with an elk leg in its mouth. Humans have no market on poverty. On despair. On the loss of hope. Animals do not name these things. They do not dwell in them as ideas, or rage against them, or give up. But the look in their eyes, and in their posture, is the same.

ben and jerome

ONE SUMMER, DAVID and I rode mules twelve miles from Onion Valley up to Rae Lakes in Kings Canyon National Park. Planning to spend a number of days there, we were using the mules to transport us and our gear. It was odd not to be packing the mules and pulling them, odd not to be riding Ace. It was odd to be a tourist and not a guide.

But the mules were splendid. And the outfitter was obviously as crazily in love with his mules as I had been with mine. His were bigger, most of them out of draft horses, strong and sturdy. David's was like that. A mule named Jerome. My mule, Ben, was smaller, finer boned, utterly beautiful. Naturally, I fell in love with him. The two pack mules looked like Jerome. The outfitter rode a horse.

Mules are good riding animals. Put together differently than horses—they are short-coupled: that is, they have the same number of vertebrae as a horse, but the vertebrae are shorter, so that the mule's back end is more underneath him—their gait is smoother and they are as sure-footed as an animal can be. Jerome was much like David. David is a sure-footed landscape photographer who is always aware of the views from anywhere; Jerome liked stopping at every turn in the trail to look out over the landscape. As the twelve-mile trail is largely a series of switchbacks, these stops were frequent. David likes to eat. After looking at the view, Jerome always lowered his head to grab whatever grass grew in the shelter of the curve. Even above tree-line, there was usually something. Although David has made numerous stock trips, they are much rarer than his backpacking trips and, like many occasional riders, he does not quite have the instinct to pull the animal's head up when he lowers it to eat on the trail. In fact, David, like most occasional riders, thinks the animal will appreciate being able to grab a snack. The fact that I ride behind David, constantly admonishing him to "pull his head up!" is irrelevant. My words ultimately just blend in with the cries of eagles, the chattering of squirrels, sounds along the trail, all things to take in, but nothing requiring concern. Sometimes I think about not speaking. About silence. But usually not until after I've said something.

Ben moved along smartly, but carefully. He walked the way I walk, not rushing, watchful for hazards along the trail and never stopped by them. The first couple of miles of trail climb steadily, reaching a long series of switchbacks cut into a rock wall. The last section of trail before the 11,823-foot Kearsarge Pass is a long shot across talus. When we backpacked the same trail a year earlier, I found it long, the altitude wearing. (In spite of living at 5,000 feet, the additional 6,000 feet made a difference.) Riding Ben, the trip was easy. And fast.

We did not dawdle atop the narrow pass (as we had, hiking) but dismounted and walked the animals down the steep west side. Ben watched my feet ahead of him, carefully placing his own so that they never stepped on my heels. At the bottom, we rode through forest and up the steep, long slope to 11,978-foot Glen Pass. Nearing the top, we passed two backpackers. Moving to the side to let us pass, one said to the other, "Now that's the way to do this."

"I'd be terrified," the other said.

I took that to mean he was frightened of riding, until, once again dismounted, we began the walk down the far steeper north side. The trail had been cut and blasted out of rock wall and steep talus. Often it descended deep rock steps, forcing the animals, however carefully they stepped, to come down hard on their front legs. Over and over, so that their front legs received a severe pounding, which can, eventually, lead to laming the animal. The trail, obviously built to discourage stock use in favor of backpackers, is diabolical for stock users. Yet, these animals are so willing to do what is asked of them. They did not complain. They simply stepped down and down and down.

At a spot where the trail had been obliterated by rockfall, backpackers had cut up (or down) the trail before the rockfall. No animal could negotiate the steep, narrow shortcut. We stopped while the outfitter and David built a trail. I stood with the animals, who waited patiently behind me, probably grateful for the break. I was grateful for the break. Then, one by one, the outfitter led his horse and the pack animals across the new, somewhat tenuous trail. David led Jerome. The outfitter said to let Ben go, that he would just follow the others.

But I *knew* Ben was an independent thinker. He looked at the trail, delicately turned around in an extremely narrow space, and headed back—toward Glen Pass, Kearsarge Pass, and home. I could not help but admire his thinking. He'd had enough of this trail. There seemed to him little point in continuing down even more of it. Never mind that his herd was going one way. He was going another.

The outfitter thought differently. I actually thought Ben was doing the right thing. By that time I'd had enough of that trail, too. Often in Yellowstone, Ace turned off a trail toward a campsite he knew, without being directed. He was often right. (He was *always* right that it was a campsite we had used, but sometimes we were en route to a farther camp.) I figure horses and mules know the land they travel better than we do, no matter how often we've been there. I tended to trust Ace's instincts about most things—except crossing bridges, which for inexplicable reasons, sometimes seemed out of the question to him. We worked it out.

"I'll get 'im!" the outfitter shouted, running past me up the trail. Recaptured, Ben finished the trip. It was a long trip, much longer than we or the outfitter expected. The size of the steps increased on the crippling trail. By the time we neared the level of the lakes and remounted, the animals were as tired as we were. The water we rode through on the first of the lakes must have felt good on their feet and legs. After depositing us and our gear at camp, the outfitter and the animals rode on another two miles to a campsite authorized for stock. In the morning, they rode back out to the pack station, returning to pick us up several days later.

The trip up the slope to the pass, first thing in the morning, was far easier on the animals than the trip down had been. We walked them down the dry, desert-hot couple of miles from Glen Pass to the forest, where we stopped for lunch. The descent from Kearsarge Pass, easier than the other descents, was rideable until we reached a long stone-and-boulder section of the trail, over which we walked the animals. And then down and down and down toward the pack station. Just before the pack station, a creek crosses the trail. Ben and I, riding tail, as we had on the way up, were free to take our own time. The creek was out of sight of the pack station cabin and corral and the truck parked beyond. It flowed through a cool, green place on a hot afternoon. A cool, green place after a long, dry day. Ben stopped to drink. He drank a long time. It was a time he and I shared. It was a time before remembering he was not my mule and I would not see him again and our time together was over.

flicka

❧

FLICKA IS *MY* horse and she has been stolen. I don't know if horse-stealing is still a hanging offense in Montana, but I intend to check on that. Punishment, revenge—these are not proper attitudes for a student of Buddhism, but they are what I am feeling. I'm supposed to acknowledge the feeling and let it go. So far, I've gotten to the acknowledging part.

Flicka was two days old when I first saw her, all legs and a tail that went *flick, flick, flick.* Flicka, her name is, I thought. Flicka. Weeks later, I read Mary O'Hara's classic book *My Friend Flicka.* Probably every girl child in America, except me, has read that book since it was first published, in 1940. *Flicka* means "little girl" in Swedish. The Flicka in the book is a young, wild filly whom the boy, Ken, loves and for whom he is responsible. Around horses his entire short life, Ken recognizes Flicka as something different from the other horses. In recognition born of love, he feels how completely Flicka belongs to him. She is his "own because of her wild beauty and speed, his own because his heart burned within him at the sight and thought of her, his own because—well, just his own." My Flicka is a sorrel like Ken's Flicka. I feel the same way Ken feels.

When it was time for her to foal, Freckles, the Appaloosa who is my Flicka's mother, was moved from the land on which the herd ran to an enclosed pasture across the road. The pasture belonged to the man who kept an eye out for the herd, calling either the outfitter or me when he noticed a problem. His pasture was a smaller place, a safer place for her to foal, one where she could be easily seen. When the man woke one morning in July, the baby was there.

Freckles and her baby were brought into a large corral just behind the man's house, where they could be fed and watered and contained enough that I could spend time with her. Champ, my accident-prone colt, who was getting special attention for whatever his current problem was, was in the corral as well. One day, when Flicka was about two weeks old, I opened the gate to the corral, closed it behind me and crossed the dry ground to her, close by her mother.

I know that every gate around horses must *always* be latched. I left the gate unlatched. As I approached Flicka, Champ nosed the gate open and left. Flicka, seeing this, ran across the corral and followed him. Freckles followed Flicka, but I got to the gate soon enough to close—and latch—it with Freckles inside. I thought that Freckles on the inside might be incentive to Flicka to return. Flicka felt no such incentive. Now I had two untrained horses happily chewing the lovely green lawn around the man's house, one a three-year-old colt, the other a two-week-old baby.

Nobody was home at the house.

～

IT WAS A gentle summer day, the sort of day when the air is a caress and the world is soft. It is the kind of day when you want to lie on green grass under an old shade tree and do absolutely nothing. Just be. Just watch clouds. Smell grass and farm fields and the rich warm scent of horses. Listen to the sound the stream makes, rippling its way down a meandering bed to join the Madison River on its way to Three Forks and the beginning of the Missouri. It is the kind of day when you join with the day, and there is no separation between you and time, you and the earth. Lying on green grass, you do not remember separation.

I attempted to herd the horses back toward the corral. I got them close, opened the gate, and lost Freckles, who had been standing there, waiting for an opening. Freckles jogged off to the yard for the good green grass. The young horses followed. Grabbing halters and lead ropes, I headed toward Freckles, who would be easiest to catch. I thought Flicka might follow her. In movies and books, babies always follow their mothers. Flicka did not. At two weeks, Flicka had her own life. She had no concept of insecurity.

～

FOR OVER TWENTY years, Freckles had been the outfitter's lead mare, ruler of the roost, the horse all other horses looked to for direction. Although she was old now, and not used on pack trips, she still commanded the herd. Flicka, who had not yet seen the herd, whose only concept of other horses was her mother and Champ, instinctively knew this. She already knew she was born to the head lady, that her birthright was leading, not following. Not even following her mother. Not even as a baby.

In the corral, I tied Freckles to a post and went back to get Champ. Champ was used to me, and halterbroken, but if he decided this was time to play, I would not have an easy time. He did. Loping across the lawn, kicking up his heels in the pure fun of feeling green grass beneath his hooves, he watched me move, teasing me with every change of direction. Flicka ran wherever he ran, probably not entirely certain of the game but aware it was wonderful. When it finally occurred to me to turn my back on Champ and walk away, he came up behind me, nuzzled me in his attempt to go on with this marvelous game. Easily slipping his halter on, I returned him to the corral, tying him to a post near Freckles. Flicka, now, was out there on her own. This seemed in no way alarming to her. She made no move toward the corral. She simply ran this way and that across the grass, which must have felt like a soft carpet to her. Freedom was natural to her. I wondered if it would occur to her to take off and run down the road. I got behind her. She ran ahead then circled back to end up behind me. I could not head her toward the corral where, now, with the other two horses tied, I had deliberately left the gate open in the hope that she would enter. Circling around the outside of the corral, she stopped to acknowledge her mother and Champ, skittering away whenever I came near.

Leaving her, I drove down the hill to the neighbor about a quarter mile away. The neighbor was a retired English professor who told me he had no idea what to do about a horse. I said he didn't need to know anything. He just had to provide another body so we could funnel her into the corral. Uncomfortable, but a gentleman, and unwilling not to help, he returned to the corral with me. Flicka was eating the lawn. We approached her on both flanks, then ran toward her so that she was directed more or less toward the corral. This also seemed an amusing game to her. She led us around the corral until, suddenly, she just walked through the gate. I closed and latched it quickly. She walked over to Freckles and began nursing. I untied Freckles. I untied Champ. I put their halters back in place and thanked the neighbor, who looked befuddled that anything had worked and walked back down the dirt road to his own house.

Not long after that, I moved Freckles and Flicka to a friend's pasture nearer my house so that I could easily spend daily time with her. I began working with her in the round pen. I ran with her in the pasture. I fed her and brushed her and loved her. When she was four months old, she returned to the land where the horses ran and was put into a fenced-off area with Ace and Champ, both of whom were being fed special food. My three horses became a unit. When Flicka was old enough to join the outfitter's herd in which she would live, Ace introduced her, as if she was his filly. He had become her protector.

Now Champ is dead and Ace is too old to work and the outfitter, nearing retirement age, sold the outfit to a young man, a former student of his. When I spoke with the outfitter on the phone about the pending sale, he told me that Ace and Flicka, along with a few of the old horses, were not part of the deal. I believed him.

After the sale was consummated, I spoke with him again. The buyer only wanted the younger horses, he told me. He let Flicka go with the younger horses. Apparently he had not mentioned she was not his horse to sell.

The outfitter loved the business. He loved the horses. He loved the wild country. He was extraordinary at the work. Outfitting is glorious and exhausting and requires all of your heart and soul and energy to make it work. And one day you are old. And the heart for it isn't quite there anymore. The heart to ask of old horses what you can hardly ask of yourself. When he felt it was time to leave the business, he talked to a therapist, to be clear he was doing the right thing. "Is your passion for the business, or for the *idea* of the business?" she asked him. Understanding it was for the business, he knew it was time to let the business go.

Good as he was at the work, he was equally dismal at the administration of the business. Details—like being on time, or selling another person's horse—escaped him. These details had caused him problems all along. Selling the business was not a high. There was no triumph in it. He got from it what he could.

"It was a mistake," the outfitter said, "for him to take only the young horses. The old ones know the business. The old ones teach the young ones. The old ones take care of you."

He was saying it was a mistake for the buyer to want Flicka because she is a young horse. He was saying he had to sell her because he wanted to get out and he wanted some money and he had misrepresented her as his horse, part of the herd.

It was I who had left her as part of the herd.

I WANT FLICKA used well. I want her ridden by someone who knows horses. I want her ridden with a snaffle bit by someone who knows how to rein with a snaffle bit because that is kinder on her mouth. I do not want her ridden by a series of neophytes, as most of the guests are. She has not yet been used on trips. She does not know the country. I want her cared for with special care. I want her properly taught. I do not want her ruined. I do not want her fearful. I do not want her sold out of the outfit. I want to know that these things will be done. This is what I want to tell the buyer.

I phone him often. He does not return my calls. The outfitter has finally let him know that Flicka belongs to me. Perhaps he is afraid I will take her away. He will not give me the chance to tell him that is not my intention. He will not give me the chance to talk about her with him. The outfitter assures me the buyer is a good cowboy, a conscientious stockman, good with the horses and the business, but shy, in need of a little more experience with people. The outfitter's genius was a skill with people equal to his skill with the stock. If this cowboy cannot make his business work, he will end by selling it. Or selling the horses. I want to make sure Flicka is not sold; not ridden by inexperienced riders; not mistreated in any way, even unintentionally; not sent the way of some ordinary horse who, old, ends up at the cannery. That's what most outfitters do. Horses who have worked their hearts out for the outfitter and who deserve a quiet retirement on good pasture are sold to the cannery for a few dollars. Dog food. "It's business," those outfitters say. "Can't keep a horse that doesn't work," they say.

I won't allow that to happen to Flicka. I will find out where she is and get her out of there. It is easy enough to find a horse in Montana, where—except for the influx of strangers into the chic cities—everybody knows somebody who knows somebody who knows where the horse is. I will single-handedly rescue her. I will ride her into the sunset. Like any proper cowboy would.

wolves in the moon

꒰꒱

A COUPLE OF years ago, David and I went to Yellowstone for several February days at the time of the full moon. David wanted to photograph a winter eruption of Old Faithful against the moon. I just wanted to be there. We had lived in New Mexico for two years and I missed the ease with which I once just drove down to the park anytime I pleased. I missed the depth of winter Yellowstone offers; its silence; the glitter of light on snow; the deep, white cold that enfolds you like an embrace. I am a northerner.

The snowcoach deposited us at Old Faithful Snow Lodge in the late afternoon. With less than an hour of light left, and the geyser soon to erupt, David waited near it with his camera while I headed out into the geyser basin toward Solitary Geyser. Solitary Geyser sits by itself on a hillside across the Firehole River from the multigeysered basin, looking down upon it like some royal, isolated kin. Part of the boardwalk crossing the basin was covered by slanting ice, a tricky few steps to negotiate. I was glad when the boardwalk ended and the trail through forest began. Deep snow lay on both sides of the trail. The trail itself was firmly packed by the feet of snowshoers and walkers. This late in the day, I had it to myself. Intending to go only as far as Solitary Geyser, I decided, once I was there, that I could easily continue to Observation Point—a popular short walk in other seasons because it offers a terrific view of Old Faithful erupting, as well as much of the surrounding country—and still return to the basin via a steeper, switchbacking trail before dark.

Lowering sun cast strips of gold between trees on the deeply forested slope. Dark shadows of snow-heavy trees framed the gold. Snow crunched under my boots. Warmed by my hurrying walk, I was comfortable on the trail, joyous in the winter landscape, grateful to be away from the few tourists below, who were waiting for the next eruption. Passing the junction with the switchback trail, I reached Observation Point at full dusk without time to linger if I wanted to return to Old Faithful before dark. At that moment, a wolf howled. Looking in the direction of the howl, I saw a brilliant yellow light at the edge of a hill. Although we had chosen the time deliberately, it took me a while to realize the light was the rising moon. The wolf howled again. A second wolf answered. The howls echoed off the moon. The moon expanded, rounded, freed itself from the hill, entered sky. I knelt in the snow, weeping with the huge beauty of the place.

I had come upon perfection. There seemed to me no further reason for anything. Here was all that had ever been necessary. I wanted to stay with the wolves, the moon, the depths of the winter night, to stay in that place and that moment forever.

How long was it before I felt the cold? The temperature, in the low single digits when I started, had sunk. Cold, I remembered the necessity of moving, of returning to Old Faithful. Maybe if I just dug down deeper into the snow. . . . It occurred to me that David would worry. Reluctantly, I rose, retraced my steps down the path to the switchback trail junction. It was full night now, but the way was broad and clear, easily visible in the moonlight. I jogged down it, feeling pleased with myself for having been present to an ultimate Yellowstone experience.

Because I had spent most of seven summers in the Yellowstone backcountry before moving to New Mexico, much of its remote backcountry is familiar to me. At home there, I have had many "ultimate" Yellowstone experiences. Even skiing, I have always entered the park at Gardiner, skipping Old Faithful entirely, so I had never walked any of the trails around the heavily touristed Old Faithful. In any season. It was an act of snobbery, of elitism. Yet the wolves and the full moon and the winter night were as deep and full an experience of wildness as any I had had anywhere in my years in the park. I was feeling privileged. And invulnerable.

~⌒

AND NOT PAYING much attention, because the trail was so easy.

~⌒

UNTIL I LOST it. I missed a turn. Realizing it at once, I climbed back up to look for it, annoyed at having to backtrack when I was rushing, but figuring it would be easy to find in the full moon. A trail that wide doesn't just end. Reaching the spot where I had left the trail, I still could not see where it went. I was reluctant to climb all the way back to the trail between Observation Point and Solitary Geyser to return the way I had come, because I was already so far down the switchback trail. Besides, I did not want to negotiate that icy boardwalk in the dark. Thinking I saw old ski tracks in front of me, I decided to walk them down through the snow, then follow the river to the bridge.

I know better than that. Within a few steps, I was ensnared by snow up to my hips. One foot did not touch bottom. I tried to turn and crawl back out. My arms simply swam without gaining purchase. I was close enough to the solid snow I had just left that there was no reason for anxiety, yet panic rose in me. It subsided as quickly, but in that instant, I understood how even experienced outdoorspeople can make mistakes that are deadly. And worse—stupid.

Few things strike me as so ignominious as dying out of stupidity. To die on Observation Point in the absolute peace offered by the magnificence of the wolves and the moon would be a gift. To die a couple of football fields away from Old Faithful out of stupidity would be idiotic. I turned slightly to one side, found enough support to push myself forward and crawl out of the snowhole, made my way upslope until I found the trail again, followed it to the trail to Solitary Geyser, descended from the geyser through forest shot with moonlight to the icy boardwalk, finessed it, returned to Old Faithful and found David who, deciding I was lost, was out looking for me. Or, at least, hoping I would turn up.

When we went into the lodge for dinner, I ran into an old friend, a biologist who spends considerable time observing Yellowstone's wolves. "I was listening to wolves on Observation Point," I told him. "Then I got lost coming down."

"The wolves would have found you," he said.

the bishop duck

꘎꘎꘎

IN THE COURSE of a stint as artist-in-residence in Rocky Mountain National Park, I was driving across Trail Ridge Road early in the season to see if some trails were snow-free and hikable. The 12,183-foot-high road crosses the alpine tundra of Rocky Mountain National Park. People were parked at pullouts all along the road. Some marveled at the views. Others were occupied by throwing chips and cookie bits to ground squirrels and gray jays. A day earlier, a ranger had talked to me about the problems of getting visitors to stop feeding wildlife. Signs didn't work, she said, nor did any amount of contact with rangers. A study had been undertaken to determine whether eating Twinkies caused problems for the jays. The ranger thought the study would at least provide solid information that rangers could offer people feeding wildlife. Something on the order of "Your Twinkies are killing our birds." But nothing made any difference. "We don't know what to do anymore," she said.

Feeding wildlife conditions animals to human food, which does not contain the nutrients the particular wildlife needs, and habituates it to human presence. A lot of food can cause soaring birthrates, producing too many of the particular animal for the available habitat. It can keep animals from gathering and storing their own food for winter, causing starvation during the seasons when tourists are not present. It makes beggars of animals who become, ultimately, pests. It can cause serious injury to hikers or campers when a large carnivore insists on claiming human food brought to the area. It can cause the death of the animal, because a habituated animal is dangerous to humans. "A fed bear is a dead bear" is no idle saying.

I stopped at an overlook for the view. An elderly couple drove their RV into the same overlook and climbed out of their vehicle. The man carried a bag of Fritos. As the two of them sat down on the wall between the parking area and the edge of the long, steep slope, a dozen gray jays descended to the wall. Several ground squirrels appeared. Birds and squirrels, edging nearer and nearer the couple as the man opened the bag and scattered Fritos on the pavement, grabbed them at once. The man threw more.

When a ground squirrel ran up the man's pant leg, the man put a Frito in the squirrel's mouth. He threw some to the others waiting on the pavement. There was no question about the pleasure the couple took from feeding. I did not want to interfere with their fun, their sense of connection, their sense of being important to these animals. It was easy to see they interpreted the animals' excitement about the food as interest and communion with them. I felt a surge of love for them, love and pity. But I could not ignore what was happening to the animals. Feeling it imperative to speak, I decided they would hear the love behind my words.

"I'm so sorry to interrupt you," I said, "but, you know, feeding wildlife robs it of interest in finding its own food, which it needs when you're not here." There, I thought, nobody could take offense at that . . .

"We've been feeding them for years," the man said. "They like it."

The woman pushed at the man's arm with her hand. She stared at me. She said nothing.

"They need this food," the man said.

"They need to find their own food," I said.

The woman tugged at the man's shirtsleeve. "Let's go," she said.

The man dumped the rest of the Fritos onto the pavement, looked at me with intense dislike, crumpled the bag with as much drama as possible and walked to the RV. His wife followed. The birds and squirrels rushed to the scattered Fritos. The couple backed out of the parking area. I turned and watched clouds over 14,255-foot-high Longs Peak and all the high Rocky Mountains surrounding it. Nobody had a good time.

When I saw people feeding squirrels in front of a sign reading "It Is Illegal to Feed Wildlife" at a picnic area in Yellowstone, I asked if they had noticed the sign behind them. They looked at it and walked away.

A friend told me about people she knew who were eating at a backcountry campsite when a fox, begging, walked into the middle of the circle they had formed as they ate. Experienced outdoorspeople who would not feed wildlife, they chased the fox out of camp. The next day, as they were eating lunch before leaving the site, the fox returned carrying a rabbit in its mouth. It dropped the rabbit in the center of their circle, then looked at them expectantly. They gave him a sandwich in exchange for the rabbit.

David and I were having a picnic lunch at a city park in Bishop, California, across the town's main street from a bakery and restaurant that makes great sandwiches. The park, with its shade trees and small, dancing stream is a cool and restful place in Bishop's desert-hot sun. A large flock of ducks had found their way to this oasis. They floated quietly in the stream or rested on the cool grass of its banks. Or begged.

Not long after we settled ourselves at a picnic table, the ducks, led by the largest of them, began making the rounds of the tables. At each of their stops, people fed them. The ducks scrambled to pick up scraps, sometimes squabbling with one another until the next tidbits were thrown. It was only a matter of time before they reached us.

We were halfway through our lunch when they arrived, the head duck looking expectantly up at us, the rest standing—with a certain amount of deference—behind.

"I don't feed wild animals," I said to the duck. "I would really *like* to, but I just can't do it. You *need* to find your own food." I knew how stupid it was, even as I spoke to him. In the face of all the scraps they were given, year after year, what I had to say was meaningless. Also, I had never actually spoken to a duck before. A friend of mine in Montana had a number of ducks, one of whom she'd named Ruth. I felt a certain kinship with that duck, but I'd never spoken to it.

The head duck listened for a moment, but while I was still talking, it stretched its neck upward so far it practically became a swan. At the top of its reach, it tilted its bill skyward while turning its head over its shoulder and pointedly away from me, turned and waddled off, followed by the entire flock.

~

I'VE NEVER HEARD of anyone else being snubbed by a duck.

yogi

⌒✤⌒

YOGI IS A boxer. He looks tough. He acts tough. He is not always rational. I had been warned that you can't trust him, that he can turn at any time. I have never been afraid of dogs, but I was afraid of him.

Yogi is companion to David's daughter, Zandria, her husband, Bobby, and their female boxer, Lucy. Lucy is an easy dog, loving, amenable, smart. I have cuddled with her on the couch in Zandria's house while Yogi was outside, contained by stout fencing.

"I'm bringing Yogi," Zandria said, when she called to give us the timing of her visit to New Mexico.

"That's fine," I said, lying. All dogs are welcome in my house, but I wished this one was not coming. I did not know how to handle having as a guest a dog who frightened me. But my relationship with Zandria was new. I wanted it to have a chance. I could not say to her that I was frightened of her dog.

Zandria, like her father, is a photographer. His subject is

landscapes. Hers is dogs. With a slate of dogs to photograph in various parts of the state, she used our house as a central starting point and a chance to visit her dad. David and I outfitted the guest house for her arrival. I put a huge, fluffy dog bed on the living room floor, so Yogi would feel welcome. I went to Three Dog Bakery and bought him a large, bone-shaped cookie that said "Yogi" on it in blue, and a blue ball I found among the toys there. I wanted him to like me. I wanted him not to be irrational. I wanted not to be scared.

"Don't look him in the eye," Zandria said, when she and Yogi arrived. I patted him on the head, talking to him with my head determinedly turned away. It was an odd way to talk to someone. I know that if I ever encounter a grizzly bear, I should not look it in the eye, but talking to a dog is like talking to a person. You need to look at him. You need to respond to him. You need to be present. You need to let him see your response. It is your expression that says who you are, not your words. Nothing feels so absent to me as someone who talks at me without looking at me. I know other cultures react differently, but Yogi is an *American* dog. He grew up in *my* culture. How would he know who I was if I didn't look at him?

I could not, however, ignore Zandria's instructions. Turning away from Yogi when I spoke to him felt odd, but I was afraid that if I looked *toward* him, I would, inadvertently, make eye contact, which he would see as a threat and instantly rip me into pieces. It would happen too fast for Zandria to call him off. We went into the house where Yogi noticed the ball on the dog bed, picked it up, and began playing.

"He loves balls," Zandria said, adding that he probably wouldn't use the dog bed. He preferred her bed.

When I was growing up, our German short-haired pointer, Rex, was not allowed on furniture. Whenever we left the house, my parents covered sofas and easy chairs with smaller chairs and books and tables. I guess we never left in a hurry. Rex—and every other dog on earth—could work her way around these inconveniences, but there was illusion to be maintained. When my ex-husband and I got our wirehaired terrier, Rex, I said he would not be allowed on the furniture. (I was a good daughter.) My ex-husband agreed. After Rex had lived with us for two days I came home one afternoon to discover my ex-husband teaching him how to jump on the bed. As I got used to sleeping with Rex (which took one night), I realized that, although my parents were right about most things, they were wrong about where a dog belongs. There was never even a thought about it when Blue came to live with me. Dogs belong on the furniture. This was corroborated sometime later by a fashionable home magazine in which various hot-shot New York interior decorators were photographed with their dogs on expensive furniture. The cover featured a designer and his four or five large white dogs on an exquisite white sofa. So, of course, I agreed with Zandria, although I thought Yogi might also like to know there was a place that was exclusively his.

Yogi paraded around the room, the ball in his mouth, proudly showing it to Zandria, to David, and to me. It was, obviously, the most extraordinary ball in the universe. I felt quite proud of my good taste. When he came to me, he seemed so much an overgrown puppy that I patted him along his shoulder, a little more enthusiastically, a little less frightened of him. Petting him on his shoulder kept me out of line with his eyes. He seemed to like the petting and I did more.

Each time I saw him, I talked to him more, petted him more. He allowed me into Zandria's truck with no fuss. As I began to feel more and more comfortable with him, I had to increase the effort to not look him in the eye.

"He can turn at any time," David warned me.

"He's not entirely rational," Zandria said.

Don't look him in the eye, I repeated over and over to myself like a mantra. Don't trust him.

Yogi was six months old when he came to Zandria and Bobby. The first few weeks and months of a dog's life teach him what life is. What had happened in that time? What had formed him, this dog who seemed so playful and eager for affection and yet, after years with caring people, was not be trusted? I began to see him not as crazy and untrained, but as possibly hurt by his first experience of life. Many good dogs are ruined by their beginnings. Shelters are filled with them. Sometimes they luck out and good people provide them with good lives, and all the bad stuff gets turned around. Sometimes they are too seriously damaged by life.

I spent more time with him. I played with him. I petted him. I looked at him now when I spoke to him, although I tried to focus somewhere around his neck. Sometimes I forgot and looked—for an instant—into his eyes. There was such longing in his eyes.

~⁓

"THANK YOU FOR not being afraid of him," Zandria said.

~⁓

How MUCH IT means to know your animal is seen for its beauty! I wanted to hug them both.

~

WAS MY FEAR gone? Wouldn't Zandria, as sensitive as Yogi, have picked it up if I was fearful, if I was just pretending to not be afraid? I am not a brave person. I have turned back from rock climbs out of fear. I have avoided social and professional gatherings out of fear. I have gotten out of the truck and walked an occasional crumbling mountain track out of fear.

Until Yogi, the only fear I had ever worked through was my fear of horses. Loving their beauty, I had been terrified of their size, ever since my father first put me on a horse when I was two. Half a life-time later, desperately wanting to ride, I was taken through fear by the horses themselves. Learning to be alert to whatever my horse might do, I rode through fear and out the other side.

With Yogi, I went through my fear because I so much wanted things to be right. I think Yogi wanted things to be right, too. Certainly, he— like the horses—took me through my fear in his responsiveness to me. If Zandria had called to say she would not be bringing Yogi, I would have been relieved. *Thank you, God, that I do not have to be around that dog.* If my only experience of Yogi had continued to be an occasional visit to Zandria's house, with Yogi fenced in, I would have missed the entire dog. Without the connection with Yogi, I would have had no real sense of Zandria. I would have missed connection with a wonderful dog and a beautiful woman. Perhaps fear is only a block when you do not want something enough. Perhaps it is a test, a message not to waste your time on things that do not really matter.

While she was here, Zandria made a photograph of Yogi standing in the doorway of the guesthouse. His house. Framed, it now hangs in the entranceway. So everyone who enters will know that this is Yogi's house.

the gorillas in the rio grande zoo

❧

I READ IN the Albuquerque newspaper that a baby gorilla had been born at the Rio Grande Zoo. The baby's eight-year-old mother, Hope, who came to the zoo in Albuquerque from the Los Angeles Zoo when she was four months old, was caring for it. Hope, hand-reared, had been introduced to the other gorillas at eight months and began living with them when she was a year old. Because hand-reared, captive-born gorillas who have never seen other gorillas care for babies, as they would in the wild, usually have no idea what to do, Hope's care of her baby was a monumental event. I had just been reading Susan McCarthy's wonderful book *Becoming a Tiger*, in which she writes about the need for mother gorillas to learn by watching—either other gorillas or humans. Hope was, so to speak, a rare bird. It seemed essential to visit the zoo.

My friend Gena, David, and I drove down to the zoo on a cool December morning. At the Marcus group compound—named for the silverback, the male, whose territory this is—Hope held Hasani, the new baby, in her big hand. In Swahili, *Hasani* means "handsome."

None of the animal keepers at the zoo speaks Swahili, but the name is perfect. He is *very* Hasani. She carried him everywhere in her hand, where he fit perfectly. When walking on all fours, gorillas place their knuckles on the ground, which leaves the palm open, facing backward. A gorilla's palm is a lovely nest. The baby seemed part of her hand, an extension of her palm.

There were other gorillas in the compound, but we were so mesmerized by the beauty of Hasani, the beauty of Hope, that we could not take our eyes from them. The few other people who walked by stopped long enough to notice the baby and went on. We stayed. Other gorillas moved around. Three-year-old Mushudu, the first gorilla born at the Albuquerque zoo in twenty-six years, tried to amuse himself with sticks, with rolling down a little hill. He looked everywhere for something interesting to do. He walked over to Hope, as if hoping the baby, his half-brother, might play with him. Hope rose from her seat on the ground and walked away, shielding the baby from him. It's tough to be an only child in a gorilla compound, no one your own age to play with. Marcus came out from behind a shield wall, built to hide the entrance to the indoor area. (Sometimes the gorillas retreat behind it when they've have enough of people standing at the railing.) Marcus is Mushudu's father, Hasani's father. He took note of all that was happening in the compound, sat down against a back wall, and watched.

Part of the celebration of Mushudu's birth was a public naming contest. *Mushudu,* which means "lucky" in Swahili, won. I don't know if this child is lucky. No one plays with him in the yard.

But Marcus is good to him. Inside, Marcus plays with him. If

Mushudu takes Marcus's food, Marcus does nothing. If one of the females takes his food, Marcus hits her. I see Marcus watching Mushudu all the time. Eventually Mushudu will grow up, become a silverback, and be moved away, because there cannot be two silverbacks in a troop. I wonder if Marcus will miss him.

When Mushudu was born, his mother, Matadi, did not nurse him for the first forty-eight hours. The primate staff was concerned because if she did not nurse within fifty-six hours, it would be necessary to take Mushudu to be hand-reared. Hand-rearing is not ideal, but it beats the alternative of letting the baby die. At the time, one of the gorilla keepers was a nursing mother. She brought her baby to the zoo and nursed in Matadi's presence. "I don't know if that's what did it," she told me, "but Matadi began nursing after that." It was because Hope had watched Matadi that she knew what to do with her own baby from the very beginning.

Within the 5,250-square-foot gorillas' yard, there is a variety of environments. (There are actually two yards here, similar in size, so the zoo can house more than one group of animals. Separated by a wall, each of the yards is about 111 feet wide and about 82 feet from front to back.) A big cottonwood grows on the east side of the Marcus group yard, its lower trunk encircled by electrified wire mesh to keep the animals from climbing to the highest limbs, then jumping to the top of the wall surrounding the yard, and out, into the greater world (or into the yard of the orangutans next door). Three old snags, anchored into the yard with bolts, offer climbing possibilities without access to the wall. In the center of the yard is a large, elaborate wooden play structure (one might call it a jungle gym) with a heavy net hammock slung beneath it. A moat (without water in it)—fifteen feet wide and about twenty feet deep—separates the front of the yard from the sidewalk where viewers stand. The side of the moat near the viewers is a sheer, unclimbable vertical wall, but the side abutting the gorillas' yard is slanted, allowing them to climb down into it and back out. From the sidewalk, you cannot see into the moat, so it offers another refuge from people for the gorillas. And from each other. The yard is surrounded by a wall of shotcrete, molded like a steep, curving cliff.

While David moved to a windowed area giving a different view of the yard, Gena and I stayed glued to the railing. Twenty-five minutes later, Marcus had had enough of us. We were too suspicious, just standing there, not moving, focused on the baby. He roused himself, ran upright along the wall to the west, gathered a handful of earth from the corner, ran across the front pounding his chest, threw the fistful of dirt directly at us so that it landed on our feet, completed his chest-thumping run across the front of the compound, and returned to the spot along the wall where he had been sitting.

In the same moment that we both understood what we had done, that we had been threatening in our staring, our insistence, our continued watching, I also was awed by the magnificence of this animal, his powerful beauty, his raw and absolute communication. We moved back and then away.

It was our introduction to gorillas.

~

I HAVE BEEN back often since that late December day. But now I sit on a bench at the back of a raised, brick platform, facing the yard yet removed from it. I watch the gorillas through binoculars. Sometimes people get in my way, but no one ever stays long. They are amused by the gorillas and try to figure out family relationships. They compare particular animals to their own family members. Most look at them as one more exhibit in a zoo, a thing of curiosity to be taken in on a visit to curiosities, although an occasional visitor is moved by their beauty. Sometimes groups of school kids tease the gorillas. They point and make fun of them. When this has gone on too long, Marcus, helpless to protect his family from their taunts, bares his teeth and throws clods of dirt. The kids, unconscious the gorillas are aware and feeling beings, find this funny. And nothing is learned.

From the bench where I sit, I have close-ups through my binoculars. I see every nuance of expression on the gorillas' faces. Every emotion registers. Without my binoculars, I see the larger view. The bench and the brick platform are dotted with bird shit. Crows roost in the cottonwood tree above the bench. I check for crows before I sit down. School children climb back and forth over the wall behind the bench until some zoo official happens by and tells them not to. They are like Mushudu, eager for some action.

Lately, I have been watching the grass green up. It is not long before new cottonwood leaves will begin unfurling. A few days ago, I watched Hope, Mushudu, Matadi, and another female, Tusa, pick leaves of the fresh new grass to eat. Marcus sat in his usual place, against the wall at the back with his eye on everything that happens among the gorillas, among the people looking at gorillas.

Lina sat by herself. She sat on brown earth, away from the new grass, picking up pieces of straw lying in the dirt, putting them into her mouth. She is a beautiful animal, but she is usually alone. Her only friendly interaction seems to be with Hope. Even when she comes into estrus, she is not interested in Marcus, and Marcus, too, leaves her alone.

Lina was hand-raised, as were all the members of the Marcus group. But Lina is shyer than the others. When she first came to Albuquerque in 1992, a keeper went into her cage with her to soothe her, people, obviously, being more comforting to her than gorillas.

There is another baby here. Ten-month-old Tulivu was born at the Denver zoo. When her mother would have nothing to do with her, she was brought to Albuquerque to be hand-reared. She was a little over three months old. (All babies born to Albuquerque zoo gorillas—regardless of where in the United States they are housed—belong to the Albuquerque zoo. Animals are often sent from one zoo to another, if one has an excess of an animal while another has a dearth. Tulivu's mother is from Albuquerque.)

Tulivu spends her days in the nursery next to the Cottonwood Restaurant. Surrounded by toys (including a couple of gorilla dolls), and tended by babysitters, she spends her time delighting visitors and staff who come to watch her through the picture window fronting the nursery. At night she goes home with the Assistant Curator of Mammals, where she has several dogs and a cat for companions. She is quite lavished with love. As Lina must have been. As each of these animals in the Marcus group must have been.

There are many of us, reared by humans and lavished with love, who dream of release into the wild, free to spend a lifetime wandering in mountains and forests, confident (to a certain extent) we could survive. But we are not gorillas. What can it be to be the center of lav-ished attention, a pampered child, and then find yourself in so radi-cally different a world? To be released into the wild, a captive animal has to be trained to survive in the wild. To be released into a zoo is different. The threats are different. The expectations are different. The knowledge of life is different.

All of these things are being considered in Tulivu's education, as she is gradually introduced to the other gorillas with whom, ultimately, she will live. Most mornings she is brought to the gorilla compound before the zoo opens for visitors. While the other gorillas are in sep-arate cages being fed, and the yard is being cleaned, Tulivu plays in the yard or wanders the hall in front of the cages, learning about goril-las. She also gets to go without her diaper. "We're treating her like a gorilla," the lead keeper, Debbie Wiese, says, "not a human."

The primate staff is trying to determine which female will be the best surrogate mother for Tulivu when she finally comes to the goril-las full time. They seem to be leaning toward Lina. By watching Hope care for Hasani, Lina is learning about babies in a proper gorilla way. She has already displayed her nurturing nature. Given a teddy bear, she cradled and loved it all day. By caring for Tulivu, Lina might become more assertive, which could improve her standing in this gorilla community. It seems a win-win situation. The next step would be for Lina to let go of her dislike of Marcus. Coming into estrus and presenting to Debbie just doesn't cut it.

When I asked Debbie how the gorillas felt about being on display, she said that to answer would be to anthropomorphize. It is hard, watching gorillas, not to anthropomorphize. We are too close to them.

There are only two chromosomes' difference between us. Nevertheless, I watch. I record actions in my notebook. I do not record ideas.

It is a warm, sunny afternoon, the first in several weeks of raw gray and rain; the zoo is more crowded than at any time I've been here during the winter. People mill on the walkways. Neon coral flamingos squawk their presence. Workers ready the restaurant and gift shop for spring opening. Beds of multicolored pansies replace the bare dirt gardens of the winter months. The warm air holds the scent of gorilla. It is not yet spring, but it is no other season either.

In spite of many visitors, the gorillas seem relaxed. Tusa sprawls in the sun near the still-bare cottonwood. Marcus sits against the wall, shaded, picking his nose, a posture Debbie describes as relaxed. Lina assumes her frequent post against the west wall. (In actual fact, Lina goes wherever Marcus isn't.) Much of the time, she turns her head away from the other gorillas, from the people at the railing. She holds her head up, as if she were a snob, but it is really just her isolation. Mushudu sits bent over the grass, studying it with utmost interest. Occasionally he picks up something and puts it in his mouth.

When I arrived, Hope was present near the front of the yard, but she left for the shelter of shade, Hasani riding—lying down—on her back. Now she leans in shade against the back wall, Hasani in her arms. When Matadi comes to her, nudging her, she retreats behind the shield wall in front of the door to the indoor cage area. When she once again emerges, the baby is hanging on to her arm. She picks up several pieces of a torn grocery bag, moves to the shade of the jungle gym, and sits with the baby. The baby nurses. Hope turns away from the people gathered. Matadi walks past her and she turns to face the front again, the sight of people, apparently, being preferable to the sight of Matadi. When Hasani is finished, she folds her arm even more protectively around him, then lies down to nap in the shade. Marcus lies against the back wall. Lina moves away from the wall to lie on her back, half in sun, one arm up parallel to both upraised legs, her hand resting in the upward position on her feet. Tusa lies in the same position on the opposite side of the yard. I try the position later, when I am practicing yoga, but my arms are too short for it to work unless I bend my knees. "Modified gorilla," my teacher suggests.

Now Matadi is lying in the sun. Mushudu lies beneath a small hill, the one he sometimes amuses himself with by rolling down. Although he is almost hidden by the hill, I can still see he is on his back, constantly moving, picking things up, putting them in his mouth—a little kid wanting to play, not nap like the old folks. Hope folds herself completely over the baby so that, unless you knew it nestled between arm and body, you would never know there was a baby.

In *The Year of the Gorilla*, George Schaller, who, in the 1950s, made the first long-term observations of gorillas in the wild, describes midmorning to mid-afternoon as siesta time. "The members of the group are pictures of utter contentment," he writes, "[...] especially when the sun shines warmly on their bodies [...] if gorillas had a religion, they would surely be sun worshippers."

Tusa gets up, picks through grasses. Matadi does the same. They are finding many things besides grass. Each morning the gorillas are provided enrichment of various kinds. Enrichment is a combination of things—cereal, raisins, peanuts, popcorn, cardboard, bamboo, river cane, paper bags—*stuff* that allows them to explore, to play, to put safe things in their mouths. (At first they were given articles of clothing, but when they were seen putting these in their mouths, that part of gorilla enrichment was cancelled. Interestingly, the orangutans next door do not attempt to eat the clothing in their enrichment packages. Instead, they drape it over themselves, or over objects in their yard.) The enrichment provided by a group of students from New Mexico State University five days a week is often elaborate; that provided by the primate staff—rushing to get the animals fed and the yard cleaned—simpler. But all of it serves to offer the gorillas things of interest to do, which, in turn, allows them to be happier animals.

Debbie told me that she (and all other zoo workers) hear disparaging comments about animals in zoos. But the fact is that most zoo animals (now) are born and reared in zoos, which is a great deal more acceptable than kidnapping animals from the wild and placing them in zoos. Even though many zoo animals have been out of the wild for generations, they still serve as a link to the wild for zoo visitors. In places like Albuquerque's Rio Grande Zoo, where appropriate minihabitats are built for them, we get a sense of who they are based on both habitat and animal. Outside of zoos, there is no such thing as one without the other. Outside of zoos, the requirements for habitat are huge. When habitat is lost—through settlement, farming, mining, logging—the animals, too, are lost. Human uses of the land displace wildlife across the planet. As wildlife diminishes or disappears, so do Earth's natural checks and balances. That nobody can live without the place that provides them a living is something humans may understand more intimately one day, but it may not matter much by that point.

Zoo animals become teachers for us. We learn from them the need to protect what remains of the wild. We learn the difference between a zoo and wilderness. If I fall in love with a baby western lowland gorilla in a New Mexico zoo, so that I become curious about what life is like for gorillas, am I not apt, then, to explore what is necessary for a gorilla's survival in its native habitat? Other zoo visitors must react the same way.

"I love these animals," Debbie says. "They didn't choose to be here. The best I can do for them is to keep them well, protect them as best I can, provide the best living conditions I can. That's why I'm a keeper."

The last time I visited the gorillas, Debbie had only half an hour to talk with me. She was leaving early for a wedding. "I'd rather talk to you," she said. "I'd rather be with the gorillas. I hate weddings."

"Just pretend they're gorillas," I suggested.

tulivu

❦

LIFTING TULIVU, I embraced a solid, beautiful baby chunk of gorilla. A muscular, spring-coiled baby with hair coarse and soft at once. She put her arms around my neck. Her body held such strength that what I felt was the solidity of her being, her absolute presence.

Tulivu was playing in the hallway when I entered the zoo office area, pulling herself up the doorknob, swinging from it, jumping down to investigate a blanket on the floor, checking out a few toys. She asked Lynn to lift her up. Lynn Tupa, the zoo's Assistant Mammal Curator, is used to her. Responsible for Tulivu's rearing ever since the baby arrived at the Rio Grande Zoo exactly a year ago, she has been working to acclimate Tulivu to the other gorillas, and they to her, since day one. This Friday, Tulivu will spend her first night at the zoo, in a cage where she will have access to Lina if she wants to be near her, and egress from her, should she choose. It will not be long before Tulivu leaves the nursery to live with the gorillas.

Lynn came to the Rio Grande Zoo from Chicago's Lincoln Park Zoo in 2001. Lincoln Park is an international leader in the management and care of western lowland gorillas, in scientific research of apes, and in involvement in the conservation of wild populations. Her mission in Albuquerque is to train animals and to teach the keepers how to train animals. She uses positive reinforcement techniques—methods that establish trust so that the animal *wants* to work with the trainer—and her training has had enormous results. Animals who once had to be tranquilized for routine visits from the vet now cooperate without the trauma of being darted with a tranquilizer. Hope was trained to receive ultrasound while she was pregnant and to hold Hasani up to be examined. In February 2005, Lynn's paper and visual presentation, "Training a Western Lowland Gorilla with the Pre- and Post-Natal Care of Her Infant," was awarded Best Behavioral Husbandry Technique by the Animal Behavioral Management Association.

"Animals work for contact or for food," Lynn says. What they respond to, and how they respond, is "*their* choice." Hope enjoyed the whole training session so much that, even after the taping of the video showing her presenting the baby to be examined was finished, she did not want to end the session. She liked the rewards.

In the hallway, I was part of Tulivu's morning exploration. Noticing me, she indicated I should pick her up. Reaching down for her, I prayed she would not be too heavy for me to lift, or slippery, or wiggly. I had no idea how much a fourteen-month-old gorilla weighs. (They are about four and a half pounds at birth.) But all of it was easy, natural, as if I held this baby all the time, although no baby feels like a gorilla. Nothing I know feels like a gorilla. I would have liked to go on holding her the rest of my life.

Later, trying to understand why holding this baby gorilla mattered so much, I came to a few parallel thoughts.

A) As animal, she personifies all the animals I have loved—that is, all animals. But because gorillas and humans share so many characteristics, she also represents some combination of animal and human, allowing me to recognize her on a level of intimate kinship. I can embrace her as I would a human baby, but she is not human. In that embrace are all beings, nonhuman and human.

B) She is the most beautiful girl in the world.

C) I am totally in love with her.

It is *not* anthropomorphizing to fall in love. It is simply falling in love. (Given my similar feelings for Hasani, it seems I have a tendency to fall in love with gorillas. "To each her own," my mother would have said.)

We walked behind the main zoo building, across pavement surrounded by the back sides of other buildings, to reach the area holding cages where the gorillas live when they are not out in their yard. Lynn slung a pink baby bag over her shoulder while Tulivu wrapped her arms and legs around Lynn's leg for the walk between buildings. Tulivu clings to Lynn the way Hasani clings to Hope's leg as Hope walks from place to place in the gorilla compound. It is how baby gorillas travel.

Because the two gorilla yards that visitors see at the Rio Grande Zoo provide an illusion of freedom, of life without bars, I was warned before leaving the offices that the holding cage area would be different. It is not odd for zoo people to be concerned about outside visitors' reaction to the idea of cages. All of us have seen the old zoos, where animals behind bars in bare cages exist as jailed curiosities on display in lost and barren lives. But Debbie Wiese, the lead keeper, had already described the cage area and I was, indeed, prepared, although in reality the cages were bigger and outfitted with many more gorilla amenities than I had imagined. These animals are treated by the keepers not as curiosities but as beautiful, vibrant fellow creatures on a shared earth.

Two howler monkeys down the hallway screamed their announcement of my presence, their voices shrill and piercing. They hung, spread-eagled, high up on the front of their cage. The gorillas rattled bars. "Stranger in hallway!" I took it to mean. I was concerned that my presence caused too much a disruption of the primate morning, but Lynn said it was appropriate for the animals to experience occasional strangers, so that a visit from the vet, or other necessary person, becomes less traumatic.

Debbie watched Tulivu while Lynn took me to meet Marcus, who, upon seeing me, ran the length of the cage, agitatedly rattling bars. A minute later, eyes demurely down, he gently accepted the peanuts I gave him. Lynn instructed me to put the front half of the peanut on his tongue so that my fingers were not in line with his teeth, then warned me never to touch a gorilla's fingers, meaning that a gorilla can grab a hand in a flash: it is a position you don't want to be in, or put the gorilla in.

~

YET TULIVU'S HAND around my arm, with all the strength and certainty of her grasp, was wonderful.

~

CAREFULLY REMOVING THE shell with his teeth, then manipulating it with his lips, Marcus spat out the shell, then ate the nut. We brought peanuts to Hope as well. Hope held Hasani with one arm while eating peanuts. Hasani, aware that his mother was getting a treat, wanted some, but he is too young for them. Lynn apologized to him for not having brought him something soft to eat.

I followed Lynn and Tulivu into a small, wedge-shaped cage between that holding Hope and Hasani and the one holding Marcus. Lina is sometimes in the cage with Hope and Hasani. Lynn pulled in a milk crate to sit on and an overturned wastebasket for me. Tulivu went on with her life, playing, eating a little baby food, climbing the cage bars, crawling into a cardboard carton in which she fit exactly. The carton was printed with the words, "Make Progress in Your Career."

On this visit, I did not take notes. I wanted simply to be present, participant rather than observer, to have nothing more than necessary between any gorillas and me. I wanted the experience, not the reporting of it. It didn't matter to me if I wrote about it or not. I just wanted whatever connection was available to me. I have watched Tulivu for hours through the nursery window. I have spent hours watching the others from the public side of the moat. Here was a remarkable opportunity to come a little closer in space to these magnificent animals. For me, the beauty of the holding area is that they are not on display. No one will ever taunt or tease them here. No one will stare at them. No one will laugh or point or say they look like somebody's brother-in-law. Even I am not watching them. I am simply present. In the same space. In a small space with a small gorilla who can touch me and whom I can touch.

While Lynn and I sat with Tulivu, the other gorillas were let out into the yard. Most of them. Marcus refused to go, because, with me present, he had no chance to interact with Tulivu. Further, he is protective of her and a stranger is a potential threat. It was not until some time after I had gone that he was willing to go outside.

Tulivu gets her own turns in the yard, chances to explore the environment that will one day be hers, but her turn is early in the day—the time I was there—while the others are still inside. Although she is becoming acquainted with the others through the cage bars, and although she will have the option of spending the night with Lina in a few days, it is still too soon for her to be in an entirely shared space with any of them.

When another keeper arrived to be with Tulivu, it was the signal for Lynn to enter the next part of her day, and for me to leave. It all happened quickly, without time for me to say goodbye to Tulivu or to Marcus. Not that it mattered to them. "Dogs don't say goodbye," Snoopy once said in a *Peanuts* cartoon. I suspect gorillas don't, either. Saying good-bye is a human event. Limiting. It ends things.

I WANDERED PAST the sea lion pool and the duck pond. A peahen with a chick on either side of her made her way down the sidewalk near the restaurant. The skinny little brown chicks strutted with the attitude of peacocks. I followed the curving walkway up to the gorillas' compound. Everybody was present except Marcus. Hope and

Hasani, Lina, Matadi, Mushudu and Tusa. Hasani, now over six months old, toddled away from Hope, exploring the large world he has discovered. Hope followed behind, never letting him wander far from her, ready to scoop him up at the first sign of danger. Occasionally, she picked him up with her large hand, placed him on her back, and moved to some other area of the compound.

It was early enough that there were few visitors. Things seemed quiet until, suddenly, Tusa jumped up and ran past Hope, swiping at Hasani on Hope's back. Hope moved quickly away and the entire yard erupted into runnings and chasings and a palpable sense of discord. Although Tusa causes discord with a certain regularity, such a rampage was something I had not yet witnessed. I wondered if it was because Marcus was not present to maintain order.

⁓

WHAT SEEMED AN innocent visit on my part had ramifications for the entire group. No act on earth is without consequence.

⁓

ON MY DRIVE home, I noticed I smelled like gorillas. I found this wonderful. I smelled like Tulivu. My clothes smelled like Tulivu. I did not change my clothes for the rest of the day.

the horses killed by lightning

TWO OF OUR horses were struck by lightning. Lying side by side at the edge of the meadow, they were still warm when we reached them. Someone tried CPR on them, but they were beyond CPR.

Dark clouds had played across the Gravelly Range since midmorning, when we moved camp; a short move across a creek, over meadows, past a rocky promontory where Jim Bridger, Kit Carson, and Osborne Russell once skirmished with the Blackfeet; downhill to the perfect meadow we had seen from the distance. The meadow offered us a short ride out to the horse trailers the next morning.

The Gravellies, in Montana's Beaverhead National Forest, form the western edge of the Madison Valley, about forty miles west of Yellowstone. We were spending four days there, doing a Leave No Trace master's horsepacking course. LNT espouses low-impact use of wild country, on horse or on foot. For anyone packing horses in Yellowstone, LNT credentials win points. Yellowstone outfitters have been required to meet high standards for low impact for a long time, but private horse users, without permits to lose, don't always measure up. Both groups are apt to ill-use national forest or Bureau of Land Management land, where there is too little ranger-power to keep tabs on how the land is treated. Low-impact techniques, like those taught by LNT, can help prevent damage.

The course was co-taught by Richard Clark, a Yellowstone outfitter with whom I worked, and Yellowstone rangers Dave Phillips and Brian Helms. There were ten students—four of us who worked with Dick; Speed, a guide from northwest Montana; a student of Dick's from Western Montana College who needed to make up coursework she had missed while competing in college rodeo; and four representatives of two chapters of the Backcountry Horsemen—one a retired U.S. Fish & Wildlife officer, one an archaeologist for the BLM.

Speed had once been hit by lightning. It knocked him out of the shelter where he slept and rolled him down the hill. Whenever storm threatened on this trip, we all teased him. "Speed, you ride over there," we would say, pointing to some far side of a meadow.

Our last camp was a good site, with lovely meadows edged by forest that offered shelter for the horses. The meadows were considerably lower than the broad, open ridge where we set up the cook tent. The ridge sloped upward, fanning out onto the forested mountain. We placed our personal tents at the edge of the fan, where it eased into forest, a good distance from the cook tent.

In the late afternoon, we gathered outside the cook tent for class time. A soft rain began. Thunder rumbled in the distance. As the thunder drew closer, we moved off the ridge, down the opposite side from the horses. The rain increased, becoming hail. Lightning cut jagged cracks down the sky. We huddled, crouching next to low shrubs and the illusion of shelter. The storm raged swiftly toward us.

I have heard that your hair stands on end before lightning strikes. As the distance between thunder and lightning lessened, I found myself waiting, sure that this time it would happen. Hard pellets of hail slid down the collar of my raincoat. When I lifted my hands to pull the collar closer, hail rolled down my sleeves. I'd left my hat in my tent, so hail pounded against my head. I was grateful to have thick hair, wondering how it would feel if it stood on end. My legs hurt from crouching so long on my heels. There was no longer distance between thunder and lightning. It was on top of us, shaking the ground, pouring itself out in ice pellets, crashing in sound through our bodies. And it hit, and we all felt it hit, and it moved on, and the hail let up, and everything stopped.

We thought the cook tent had been struck. We ran up the ridge, but it was standing. We crossed to the other side. I saw the horses grazing in the meadow. Then I saw Pepper and Sunny lying at the meadow's edge.

The sky was a clear, washed blue, as if nothing had ever happened. The storm had lasted no more than ten minutes. Ten minutes earlier, two beautiful horses were alive. The lightning must have hit one and gone into the other and blown them both from under the trees onto the grass.

Pepper was twenty-three years old. She was much younger when I rode her during the Yellowstone fires in 1988 as a guest on my first trip with Dick, and for several years afterward. In 1988, I knew little about riding horses. I had taken several equitation classes at Montana State University, figuring that if I meant to live in Montana, I'd better learn to ride a horse. Pepper was the first horse I rode outside the school arena. When I told Dick I was a nervous new rider, he said Pepper would take care of me. "She reads a rider like a book," he said. "If you want to rodeo, she'll rodeo. If you need a little help, she'll help you."

The first time we came to a fallen log, Pepper stopped, turned her head toward me to check if I was ready, then, gently and easily, she jumped the log. I stayed on. Every day I spent on her, she taught me more about riding trails. Even after I got Ace, I continued to watch Pepper take care of other people the same way.

Sunny, an eight-year-old gelding, was a big, sweet, beautiful Appaloosa with butterscotch markings, markings like the sun. All last summer, he had been ridden by another of Dick's wranglers and the two had formed a bond like brothers. This trip, Speed was riding Sunny.

The other wranglers and I stayed with Pepper and Sunny a long time. Then we gathered sage and brought it as offerings to them and moved on to each of the horses standing at the edge of the forest a short way away. We talked to them and loved them. I spent a long time with Skipper, Pepper's special friend. The two were always together in the pasture. If one went on a trip while the other stayed behind, the returning horse whinnied to the other on arriving home, and the other came running. How was it Skipper wasn't hit? He could not have been far from Pepper.

The next morning, all the horses came, in single file, to Sunny and Pepper. Skipper lay down next to Pepper. I don't know if horses understand death, but I saw them know the world had changed. When Skipper arrived home that evening, he did not whinny for Pepper.

Dave Phillips and Brian Helms offered to cut the horses open after everyone left in the morning. The retired Fish & Wildlife officer stayed back with them. And I stayed. Cut open, it is easier and faster for other animals to get to them. For other animals—bears, coyotes, eagles, ravens—carcasses mean survival. It allows the horses to become part of the chain of nature faster. I needed to see this happen. I needed to know they would not be getting up and coming out after us. I needed to see the whole thing through. I needed to know it was over.

Dave cut a single slit down each belly. The innards exploded out. He patted the horses and said goodbye to them. We walked our horses—tied a distance away from Sunny and Pepper—to the creek so Dave could pour water over himself. I thought I was calm, but, attempting to follow Brian across the creek, I suddenly could not see how to cross, although I have crossed ten thousand streams. Brian took Ace's lead rope and held out his other hand to me. On the far side, I put Ace's bridle on backward. Brian turned it around. I tightened the cinch, but not enough, so that, as I put my foot in the stirrup, I pulled the saddle over Ace's side. Dave helped me push it back. I rode exactly behind Dave, to keep Ace, who had picked up my nervousness, from loping off to reach the rest of the herd, fifteen minutes ahead of us. Some guide I am. It would have been funny if it had not happened out of heartache.

champp

❦

CHAMP'S WHOLE LIFE was an accident. His mother, Belle, was a year-old filly out in the pasture with the rest of the herd, including Coco, a year-old, ungelded colt. The outfitter never considered the two would get together. One morning, out to bring the horses in to the corral, he found a brand-new baby. Coco was gelded that afternoon.

Hardly had the new baby, Champ—Champion, after Gene Autry's horse—gotten in to the corral than he snagged his right eye on something that pulled the eyeball from the socket. The vet put it back in place and he did not lose the eye, although sight from it was limited. It sat a little lower in his face than the other eye and looked a little bigger. But there have been some great one-eyed horses. One-Eyed Jack, born without an eye and raised by a nearby outfitter, turned out to be one of the great trail horses of the region. Other one-eyed horses have raced or done dressage or worked as cow ponies. I wasn't worried about Champ having only one good eye.

Besides, he was a handsome little guy, a sorrel with a white diamond blaze on his forehead; good, strong conformation; enormous curiosity about everything. He was about six months old when he was given to me after my first season of working with the outfitter in Yellowstone. The outfitter suggested that Champ and I could learn together.

I lived in Bozeman and, at the time, the herd lived in Idaho, so I had little opportunity to work with him for the next year, although twice the outfitter brought him, my horse Ace, and the outfitter's personal horse, Topper, to Bozeman. Once, riding Ace, I trailed Champ in the Story Hills, north of town. By his second visit, my ninetysomething parents had moved to Bozeman to live with me. I have a wonderful photograph of my mother sitting in her wheelchair, in the driveway, holding Champ's lead rope and talking to him. I was charmed by watching my mother's conversation with Champ. She had a great deal to say to him. In the photograph, Champ seems charmed, too. Out of the picture, Ace and Topper are grazing the front lawn. I lived on a main street in town. Traffic stopped as it passed my house.

My father was unwilling to come outside. With a mind no longer the mind we all knew, he seemed not to remember that horses had once been his life. Growing up in New York State's countryside, he had helped his father, who was a horse trader. Later, my father taught riding in the army, at a time when the cavalry was just a frill, but, for him, a frill that mattered. I was sorry he would not come out to see the horses. He had put me on a horse when I was two, but the horse seemed so large to me, and I felt so small, I cried to be taken down. Knowing I could not ride without being ready to ride, he lifted me from the horse. Now I wanted to show him how far I had come. I wanted to show him I had my own horses. I wanted one last chance to show him he had been right to put me on the horse. It just took me a lifetime to get used to it.

My father tried to teach me to ride. Now he taught me we don't get last chances.

~⁐

A YEAR LATER, the herd was moved to seventy acres in Harrison, Montana. On almost four times the land they'd had in Idaho, they ran like wild horses. Few things are as beautiful as the sight of thirty horses running across meadows. And oh, they *ran* when they arrived, they ran when we rounded them up for a pack trip, they ran for the pure joy of being horses. Watching them was watching joy, watching the height of life, the absolute blending of earth and movement, a perfection of being.

When we gathered the herd to select those for a pack trip, Champ, Belle, and Coco entered the corral with the others, even though none of them had yet been trained for riding. I took a little time with Champ then, brushing him, loving him. When the animals not going were released back into the pasture, Champ ran with them, as eagerly as he had coming into the corral. All of it seemed wonderful to him.

Champ was four years old when we took him, Belle, and Coco to a colt-breaking workshop. I had worked him a little with a long line in the corral, but the workshop was our chance—as the outfitter had said—to learn together. The workshop was offered by a locally renowned horse-whisperer sort of trainer at an Idaho ranch.

In spite of having seen the other horses saddled and ridden, the three wild horses had no idea life would come to having some heavy thing placed on their backs, or straps tightened around their bellies. All three objected. It was only a matter of moments with them before the trainer decided that he and his assistants would do the initial work, rather than coach us in it. I think he was afraid the outfitter and I would get killed and then sue him. From heaven.

Belle and Coco presented the trainers with difficult circumstances. They (and Champ) were considerably older than the other colts, who were less resistant to the whole process. We watched the success the other participants were having. I wanted to be doing the same thing, having the same success. I wanted to be the one to train Champ. I wanted this to be between him and me.

The two men working with Belle and Coco moved carefully, patiently, completely focused on the animals. As the crowd of us sitting on bleachers outside the round pen watched, they succeeded—finally—in getting saddles on the horses. Champ also watched. Then, as the trainer turned to Champ, Champ's interest became less focused. He stood uneasily as the trainer showed him the saddle blanket, let him smell it, talked to him, gentled him into the moment. Champ allowed the blanket. The trainer went through the same process with the saddle. Champ stood for the saddle being carefully, gently placed on the blanket. He allowed the trainer to buckle the cinch. He stood quivering for an instant during which I could see refusal in his eyes. I could see decision in his eyes. Then he exploded. Bucking, sunfishing his way around the corral, he backed up, eyeing the fence surrounding the corral. The fence was close to seven feet high. Everybody saw him look, but none of us believed he would attempt to jump.

"He's not gonna do it," one of the assistants said.

And then he was gone. Running from the far side of the corral toward the fence in front of the bleachers, he left the ground, his front hooves just clearing the top of the metal fence, pushing against it with his rear legs, then falling down the other side, our side. There was a ditch there, lower than the round pen so that the distance from fence top to ground was greater on the outside than on the inside of the pen. He landed on his back in the ditch, head down, body upslope, then rolled over onto his side. He lay absolutely still. None of us moved. No one spoke. I doubt anyone breathed. Disbelief rolled over the bleachers like a wave. It rolled through each of us watching. It rolled over the corral. Nothing but the disbelief moved. Not us. Not the wind. Not time. We thought he was dead. It was so fast. He opened his mouth and began eating the grass at his mouth. I ran down to him. The trainer ran to him. He stood up, lowered his head and ate more grass. Everybody laughed. The trainer led him back into the round pen, walking him to make sure everything worked. Everything did.

After the workshop, one of the cowboys working with the trainer took Champ home with him. The cowboy spent several weeks working with Champ at the family ranch. He worked him in the round pen and he worked cattle with him. By the time I drove up to the ranch, Champ was as ready for me as any horse could be. Riding him was great pleasure. He felt strong and sturdy and willing. A week later, we took him on his first trip in Yellowstone.

However comfortable a horse may be in the ring, or in pastures chasing cattle, a wilderness trail is a different thing. It will be rife with things the horse has never seen. The experience will not compare with anything he has yet done. Yet, Champ would be with horses he knew. He would follow them in their sureness through the experience. Horses follow one another over and through places they will dispute on their own, or in the lead. Even experienced trail horses are sometimes more comfortable following the horse in front than they are being the lead horse. Champ seemed pleased to be with the other horses, interested in the new surroundings he found in Yellowstone. I saddled and bridled him with no problem. He was the same pleasure to ride he had been at the ranch.

Everything went smoothly until we came to narrow, wooden erosion bars dug into the ground across the trail. Ground-level in the trail, they contained between them a shallow ditch, a few inches across, to divert water from one side of the trail to the other. Even though I kept him close behind the horse ahead, Champ noticed everything in the trail as if he was on his own. In the cowboy's pastures, he had not followed another horse, so he had become used to seeing on his own.

Until the erosion bars, the trail had been straightforward. Now we had something new. He stopped, took a step backward, lowered his head to investigate this strange thing closely. I let him look at it. He took another couple of steps backward, gathered himself together, and leapt over it as if it had been a three-foot-high log.

The next day we came to a similar construction. He stopped at this one, too, backed up a step, and took a much lower leap over it, a gentle, floating movement. Later in the day, we came to a third one. Again, he stopped, looked at it, and then stepped over. When, in the following days, we came to more, he simply kept moving as if it was nothing in his path.

I loved his process of studying. I wondered if I learn the same way, approaching the thing I am to understand as if it is a great obstacle requiring tremendous effort to overcome, only to find, at last, that it is simply a step on the path. It is not an intellectual process; rather, an understanding in the body that carries the mind along. As the body understands, the mind relaxes enough to receive the lesson. I suspect it is the same with great dancers and athletes. I have been watching how I learn ever since that trip, so that, in every new moment I experience, Champ is present. Champ is dead, but I will ride him as long as I live.

Two years later, I married David and left Montana and Yellowstone and my beloved horses—Ace, Champ, and my three-year-old filly, Flicka. They were so much a part of the herd that it seemed right to leave them with the herd, right to leave them in that treasured landscape where they were at home, rather than bring them to New Mexico with me. Besides, David and I were traveling too much for me to keep horses. Horses require that you be there. They require that you keep careful check on what happens in the pasture, that you be present to their lives. Although the three horses were friends and would have come together, they would have had to be boarded here, their free spirit enclosed. All of the circumstances made it less than ideal to bring them with me.

~⌒

It was a mistake. I had been here a year when the outfitter wrote me that Champ had died in a freak accident, pierced by a piece of wood in the pasture. He had been taken to the vet, but it was too late. The wound had already become infected. He died at the vet's. I will never know the whole story because I wasn't there. Not being there was the mistake. Not watching those horses twenty-four hours a day was the mistake. I do not know how much time elapsed between the accident and the arrival at the vet's. How long before somebody noticed. I do not know what the piece of wood was—a branch or a twig fallen from a tree, or some piece of refuse left lying around. I only know that Champ is dead.

Riding Champ or Ace in Yellowstone, sometimes over difficult terrain, always over long miles, seeing the heart with which they worked with me, seeing the heart with which all the horses in the herd worked, makes my own heart cry. How does an animal give and give and give to you and never question his giving? You try to repay the giving with good care and good technique and a willingness to understand the language of the animal, but you know that your own giving is never so huge, so complete, as what you are given.

Champ had so much heart. He came through so much. But he could not come through this last accident. When I got the letter that he had died, I blamed myself, I blamed the outfitter, I blamed God for putting us all in this situation, because somewhere I believe it could have been prevented. I cried. I put the photographs I have of him on the wall so I can see them from my desk.

The photographs remain there. I have forgiven God and the out-fitter and, to a certain extent, myself, because the nature of accident is accident. When my father died, it was also accident. Accident caused by an irresponsible nurse. Yet, it was time for my father to go. The irre-sponsible nurse was merely death's agent, like Judas, chosen to betray Christ. The time we are given is personal. For my father, it was long. For Champ, it was short, even though, accident-prone as he was, it may have been longer than I should have reasonably expected. But I have Champ with me each time I enter the new, the beginning. Leaping hugely over the obstacle that *beginning* is, then easing into the process that is understanding, my teacher, Champ, is with me all the time.

Champion. You earned your name.

afterword

⌒❧⌒

THIS MORNING, A Cooper's hawk flew into my garden. In that instant, a dozen finches, almost as many sparrows, and sixteen Mexican doves erupted into the air. The hawk settled in the piñon in front of the kitchen window. I hoped the current crop of baby rabbits was more hidden than they normally are, lying for hours on the gravel paths or in the cool dark earth beneath the piñon or the wisteria that climbs the arbor. Yesterday, a young neighborhood cat stalked something in the grasses near the bird bath, pounced, then left the garden carrying a small gray thing in its mouth. Was it a bird? A newborn rabbit? A mouse? I haven't seen the mouse who lived under the flagstone beneath the bird feeder in weeks. Not long after the cat attack, David watched our resident roadrunner deftly stab a young bird, jump up onto the wall with the speared bird on its beak, turn to make sure David saw the magnificence of his work, then eat the bird. Oblivious to the current deaths, the pheasant who lives in the high grass of the meadow ambled beneath the apple trees; a hummingbird darted in and out of the penstemon; a lizard scurried up the wall of the atrium; small white butterflies flittered in delicate droves through the lavender; an overturned beetle in the living room waved its legs in desperate urgency to be righted (I took it outside and complied); a cricket chirped from behind the Victorian cupboard in the front hall; and the sound of coyotes singing somewhere between here and the river drifted up the meadow. Outside my workroom window, the woodpecker took his frequent position on the apple tree between the house and irrigation ditch and began pounding.

These are just things that happen. Observations. Nothing in particular. Ongoing life and death. But they make me think about my stories—also just things that happen. Animals come into my garden, come into my life. Each presents me some new moment. Each teaches me something. I may not always be able to name the lesson, but I certainly engage in the process.

～

I MOVED CLOSER to the window to better see the hawk. He flew off at once, his dark spread of wings huge against the kitchen window. In not considering the effect of movement I lost the chance to observe him, although I inadvertently did a favor for the finches, sparrows, doves, and rabbits. I was disappointed the hawk was gone but felt a certain relief all those other critters were, for the moment, safe.

In feeling relief, I lost the neutrality of the observer. A fleeting emotion turned me into a participant in the drama, although discovering myself favoring finches over raptors surprised me. How could *any* passerine come before those extraordinary wild beings who carve the air with such beauty, verve, and intention? Since when did a sparrow equal (for me) a raptor? Since when did my biases get so skewed?

Prior to arriving at The Peregrine Fund hack site, I had been sent a handbook instructing me in methods of killing the quail provided by The Peregrine Fund to feed the young falcons. It suggested the two best choices for humane killing were twisting the bird's neck or banging its head sharply against a rock, the way you kill a fish. "Can you kill?" had not been a question on the job application. My horror at the idea of killing something made me wonder if I was heading into the wrong project until, finally, it occurred to me that a parent bird kills to feed its young. In the place of a parent, I had better be able to do the same. And it was a quail, for heaven's sake, not a raptor I was being asked to kill. It was food. What kind of a parent would not kill food to feed a family? What kind of falcon did I think I was? Worried I would not be forceful enough to do the job with one bang, I chose to practice twisting.

It turned out the quail I was provided were already dead and frozen and that the handbook I had been given was out of date. I was relieved the quail were dead but I was sorry not to face—and pass—the test.

I feel this way about dead meat I buy for my own dinner, too. There seems to me something unethical about buying packaged meat, rather than taking responsibility for the animal's death. The hunter facing an animal in the animal's habitat, where death is a natural part of the animal's environment, cannot ignore the connection between him- or herself and that animal. But few people buying the literally disembodied meat at a market think about the animal's life, the fear the animal experienced at the slaughterhouse, or the fact that the animal was raised solely for slaughter.

Food is a place of connection, even if one eats unconsciously. Everything is connected through what it eats. I used to worry, as I wandered around Yellowstone, that if I were eaten by a grizzly bear and the bear was then killed, I would be wasted. If I was going to be a meal, it seemed a shame to be the *last* meal. But a dead bear (left lying where it is killed rather than hauled off to a lab to be eviscerated in order to discover what—besides me—it was eating) feeds eagles and buzzards, ravens and coyotes, so that, even as a last meal, I would become part of the chain of nature. This strikes me as a better deal than lying around underground, vaulted away from the earth for eternity.

The possibility of being eaten stimulates connection. In Yellowstone, there is no moment I am not alert to the presence of bears (no matter that I may relax my guard when they are hibernating). In Jack London's story "Love of Life," a man's connection to a wolf is a struggle between equals: "a sick man that crawled, a sick wolf that limped, two creatures dragging their dying carcasses across the desolation. [...] The patience of the wolf was terrible. The man's patience was no less terrible."

It is connection in which both man and wolf *know* the consequences of one or the other gathering strength enough for a single, defining moment. It is the connection of equals.

We share with all animals a reluctance to be eaten. (I know there are people who may never think about this.) Interestingly, though, people who choose totem animals—the animal they feel represents them, guides them, or gives them power—are as apt to choose prey animals, like the horse or gazelle, as to choose predators, like the jaguar. While nonindigenous people are likely to choose glamour animals—race horses, wolves, grizzly bears, eagles—Indians, upon being presented an animal guide in the course of a vision quest, regard all animals as noble. It was the little, modest chickadee who came to Plenty-Coups, when he was nine years old. In the text of Frank Bird Linderman's book *Plenty-Coups*, Plenty-Coups describes a dream sought through a vision quest. In the dream, he witnessed a great forest struck down by the Four Winds. One tree was left standing. "In that tree is the lodge of the Chickadee," Plenty-Coups was told. "He is least in strength but strongest of mind among his kind. He is willing to work for wisdom." The little, inconspicuous chickadee, who could alight on a slender branch in a great storm, weather the storm, move with the wind, was interpreted by the Crow elders as the model for the Crow tribe's dealing with the U.S. government in the nineteenth century. By moving with the winds of the time, the Crow suffered less at the hands of the government than did most tribes.

Chickadees come to our bird feeders in winter. The hawks are present year-round. I would like to be like the chickadee, willing to work for wisdom, able to move with the wind. I would like to be like the hawk, swift, agile, direct. As an observer, I should watch each with interest, not favor one over the other, not choose sides.

Sometimes, though, I find myself choosing both sides of the equation—at the same time partial to both the eater and the eaten. There could be a logic to this, since we (humans) are predators with a history in which we have been prey. We occasionally become prey even now. Ideally, this should equip us to see both sides of a question, but does it produce the same neutrality as that of a disinterested observer?

Predator and prey are necessary to one another. Large populations of prey species allow predators to prosper. Large populations of predators decimate prey which, in turn, causes the numbers of predators to fall and prey to rebound. In this way, the earth (left to its own devices) controls how the earth is used.

But we do not leave the earth to its own devices. There is nowhere we have not interfered with the earth's processes. Maybe the hugeness of our interference with the natural order of things is part of what prompts the focused urge toward connection with animals, the instinctive reaching for balance I discussed in the introduction to this book. Maybe it is an attempt to understand how the earth actually works. On the other hand, we are *also* part of the natural order of things. Does this mean we are supposed to interfere?

I have a problem accepting some degrees of interference. "Shoot, shovel, and shut up" is not an uncommon expression in the West, where there is a traditional animosity toward predators who can cause problems for ranchers. I know a sheep rancher who regards tending his flock as a God-given mandate. He *will*—by God—*kill* anything that attacks his sheep. I also know a cattle rancher who says the few losses of animals to predators are part of the cost of doing business. Both ranchers connect to their own animals and to predators. Differently.

So what does connection to animals mean? Is it personal and emotional, or do we experience it on some more primordial level, as I suggested in the introduction? Can it be both? Does it include all animals, or do you choose between your dog and mountain lions, between livestock and wolves, between cats and coyotes, between raptors and finches? Does understanding the necessity for wildlife and space for wildlife mean abstaining from connection to domestic animals because sometimes the needs of the two conflict? Wildlife (and land enough for wildlife) is vital to many of us. It also happens to be vital to the life of the planet.

But Blue was the best backpacking partner I ever had, and that sharing was too deep to be missed. We share the planet with wildlife, but we share our lives with dogs and cats and horses and birds. All of this matters.

Ace is old now. He is healthy, except that he no longer has the molars or incisors necessary to chew grass so that he can get nourishment from it. Without special feed, he will starve to death in the lushest of pastures. The vet told me recently that I had to decide whether to put him down or keep him on expensive senior feed for what could be years, given his otherwise good health. Because he can no longer earn his keep, most outfitters would euthanize him. But he worked too hard for too many years to be deprived of an honorable retirement. If the pasture cannot feed him, it can still offer him the pleasure of a lope through the morning dew. He can still revel in the warmth of the spring sun. Like the foal discovering it is a horse in a landscape it will never question, he can feel the earth beneath him and the sky above. Whatever time is available to him, Ace will have it, living for the pleasure of life.

All animals, wild or domestic, live because life is given to them. Only we question the meaning of life. Our questioning is entirely human, but it is guaranteed to remove us from the present moment.

When, in the story "My Dog," I recalled David's suggestion to "Let's do now forever," I was remembering an instance of total human engagement in the moment, an instance of living—like any other animal—because life has been given to us. It was a moment no different from the Cooper's hawk flying into my garden and all the other birds erupting into the air, or the wolves in the moonlight, the coyote on my skis; no different from Ace running across the pasture for the pure joy of it, or of Blue chasing with his whole being the imaginary ball. "Life *is*," they are saying. "I am here," they are saying.

∽

In living in the moment, there is no disengagement from the earth. This is what I want to learn.

∽

But ask now the beasts,
And they shall teach thee;
And the fowls of the air,
And they shall tell thee;
Or speak to the Earth
And it shall teach thee:
Job, 12: 7–8

acknowledgments

❧

SEVERAL OF THESE stories had earlier incarnations on the Leisure & Arts page of *The Wall Street Journal* in a somewhat different form. "The Dog" first appeared in *The Bark* and "In the Course of Things" in my book, *Partings and Other Beginnings*. Both these stories have been altered from earlier versions. Aspects of "Ace," "Ben and Jerome," and "Wolves in the Moon" were published in *Our National Parks*, a recent collaboration with David.

I owe great thanks to Tom Silva, Lynn Tupa, and Debbie Wiese at the Rio Grande Zoo, and Beth Dillingham at the Rio Grande Nature Center.